# Knowledge Society?
# No thank you. Or yes please!

My song to all of our fantastic societies.

A constructive criticism and a roadmap to the goal.

*"Do as you use to do, and get what you use to get"*

**Author     Kjeld Reby Loren**

Previously published by the same author:
- Keglebillard – et håndværk (Danish)
- En læreplads som keglebillardspiller (Danish)
- Booklet series Jeg vil lære! (till now - 10 education booklets on Pin Billiard and sport psychology) (Danish)

ISBN           978-87-7114-349-2
Original title Videnssamfund? Nej tak? Eller ja tak!
Translation   Kjeld Reby Loren
Cover         Kjeld Reby Loren
Illustrations Kjeld Reby Loren
Inspiration   Kjeld Reby Loren
Transpiration Kjeld Reby Loren
Print         Times New Roman
Production    Books on Demand GmbH, Norderstedt, Germany
Publisher     Books on Demand GmbH, Copenhagen, Denmark

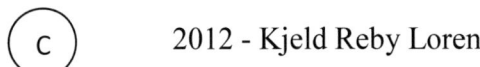
Ellinge lyng January 2012.

To my Denmark, which I love so very much.

# Table of contents

# Dear English spoken reader!

It is a great pleasure to reach out to you.
You are, however entitled to a few concessions from me.

The book you are about to read, is in the first place written to the Danish society. Therefore, I will be referring to conditions, which perhaps only are applicable in Denmark. Where it is possible, I tried with rephrasing and explanations.

The book is not written in rural, picturesque, rich English. It is written with the English language, I know. I have used the English language, as a tool, a bridge between you and me. I hope that not too much pigeon English has sneaked in.

Denmark is a country with scarce natural resources. At least as far as those, which in other countries can be dug out of the soil? But we are rich in human resources. Those, we must use. That is why a Knowledge Society important for us.

Later on, I saw, that these properties Denmark shares with many other countries. These countries are therefore all obvious candidates for the establishment of a Knowledge Society.

Right to the bone however, a Knowledge Society will be useful, beneficial and desirable for the any country. Regardless of size, natural resources and stage of development.

So dear reader: Go ahead with the book with great expectations.
I do not think that I am going to disappoint you.

# Foreword

Dear reader. To be critical and constructive is not just an author right. It is also his duty. It does not mean that all writers need to take on this obligation. So far from that. We also need authors, which are good to entertain us. We need authors, which gives us information. And authors, which do not have any mission at all. Who writes, just because they like to write, or just cannot leave it.

I have written text books to provide information to the interested parties. To convey my knowledge and experience. It has been positive, enriching for me. Hopefully also for my readers.

This book is something different. I criticize what I find is wrong. Also what I find should be done differently. My criticism would be worthless to me, if I not at the same time could show a way to changes. That is why my personal motto, which can be seen on the cover, is: *"Do as you use to do, and you will get the usual result"!*

If what you usually do is good, then keep on doing it. But if you want a change, then you have to do something differently.

A very simple declaration. So blatant obvious, that there is a temptation to call it banal. Was it just that well. If this was the recognized common opinion in our society, then there was no reason to write this book.

But that is just not the case. A preface must not be longer than strictly necessary. I just want to sharpen your appetite and tickle your curiosity . My book contains not a single reference. Nor many quotations of other clever people. And no long list of thanks to persons and institutions. It is due to the fact, that what you read, is MY opinion. Emerged from my observations, my knowledge and my experiences.

Get yourself ready to initiate a process of change.

Good appetite on your reading.

# What is wrong?

Yes – that is where it all starts. Is something wrong? Look around making your own judgements. You have to be open observing. Don't you find, that there is a lot, which does not work properly? Is there not a lot, which operates inappropriate? At least, so it is viewed upon from my position in life.

But I will in this book focus solely on the relatively new concept of *Knowledge Society.*

When I hear the word, it gives me a very light feeling of sickness. Not seriously. But enough to make me feel a little uneasy. How can that be? Is the word not positive? Yes – if priority is put behind the word. If there really were made change promotion plans. And those plans were carried out for real. And those plans were thoroughly useful. If they had weight.

It is what is wrong. All of that is lacking.

The word Knowledge Society is used most often by politicians, as a rabbit pulled out of the magicians hat. Almost as a *dealer takes it all* card. Slam it briefly on the table, and you automatically close the mouths on the critical voices. Then they have said, that they have the intention of a Knowledge Society. Some time.

It is accompanied often of a list of measures, we will take. Some time. If we get the required power. Some time. And there is the financing for it. Some time.

Look at the proposals already placed on the table. Do you see the slightest hint of guarantee, to the works? No – not really? It is almost exclusively hot air. It is keeping balloon floating. But behind the thin shell, there is no substance. Have you not heard something similar before? But it is probably a long time ago.. Do you remember the adventure of *The emperor's new clothes* by the famous H. C. Andersen? We say that the substance is there, but no one can see it.

I would like to be the little boy for you. Me, they may point the finger at and say: He do not understand. But I do. And deep in your heart I believe that you do too.

Misuse of the word is called populism. Let us not stir more in it. It is closely related to one of the other, political "in" word: timely care. Do you see what I mean?

Say the words and the criticism is silenced. But – the problems are not resolved. The positive, effective change is not created.

That is what is wrong! *We do as we use to do and get the expected result – nothing!*

Let us therefore start by focusing on what we want, and what we need – a *Knowledge Society*.

# Pseudo knowledge.

Argh – quite frankly. *Knowledge, that isn't knowledge, does not exist*. Yes it does – unfortunately.
But I agree with you, that it requires a detailed explanation. Otherwise, it would only be another fancy "in" word. Hot air. So let me deflate the balloon, so that we can actually see the real content of it.

# Course.

This is really a "swinger". Hey – I'm attending a course. You shall attend a course, Him we must have to attend a course. We are all going to attend courses. Can you – perhaps a little sceptical, hesitant, nodding recognize those statements? The course mania is existing largely in all parts of our society. In all the companies and institutions. Amongst all who has a job. And within the majority of those without a job. Just hand them a course.

Courses are also used as a reward in many places. Him, we would like to retain, so hand him a course. Be assured – he will gladly accept it. It is held in a nice hotel in Glasgow or San Francisco. With both travel an expenses paid. He will attend, happy, that the light of mercy is shining upon just him. For all sake, he is lucky. Or is he indeed?
.
Quite so many people take part in courses, they do not have the slightest interest in. They receive education – knowledge – which  they do not have any intention to use. Such knowledge is not captured. Nor is it trained, and are therefore not kept as knowledge. After a short time, it is non-existent. It has become pseudo knowledge

Ostracised are also the courses which are not timely.
Courses, given too late, are not always negative. But it is inappropriate backlog. It has for several years been in to call knowledge obtained on a

training course for a competence. A beautiful word. Main competence.
Umm – delicious.
The fact is, however, that a competence must be present, when there is a
need for it. It must not come slowly dragging, long after the need arose. This
can be seen regularly.
The swimmer is offered a boat, after he exhausted has crossed more than
half the river. May say cursing no thank you. Not loud, but silently within
himself. Such an added knowledge is pearling off like water on a goose, and
will become pseudo knowledge

The worst of the courses, which are not timely, are those given too early.
The attendant arrives with a great interest. Eagerly absorbing knowledge.
Makes a real effort. Looks forward to come back and use his new
competence. But – unfortunately two years passes, before the company is
ready to use his new competence.
This knowledge gets quite rusty, get full of holes, and passes eventually in
to the category of pseudo knowledge. This is, unfortunately often
disincentive for participation in further training courses.

So we are not getting a Knowledge Society only by increasing the course
activities. But we can approach a Knowledge Society by exclusively
offering and participating in relevant courses. Relevance in time, content
and quality. Or relevant in relation to your own, personal interests.

Pseudo knowledge is in other words knowledge, that you think you have,
you once had, or your surroundings thinks you have. But it is just not
existing anymore.

## Inherit-knowledge.

Yet another word I had to add to my text programs vocabulary.
But what does it cover? Hot air?

No. It is absolutely genuine. Apparently. The procedure is this:

A person, with many years of experience, tells you, that this is how it is!
Because so he was told by his predecessor. So, of course, you must also
know it.

But this knowledge has never been put to a test. A proof of its validity has
therefore never seen the light of day.

Of this we have numerous examples of: The earth isn't really flat? The sun
doesn't circle around the earth? You know probably several examples of
inherit or passed-down information, which does not hold water on a closer
examination.

This is a false knowledge and therefore pseudo knowledge. Real knowledge
can be proved.

## Claim-knowledge.

Again I had to add new knowledge to my text programs vocabulary. So what does this word-bastard cover?

A claim is flung out as a self-evident truth. We are talking here about truth-like allegations.

The most dangerous allegations come from people who we should be able to trust. Politicians, officials, academics and others in central key positions in our society.

They have often easily recognizable symptoms like, for example the initiation of a claim. Here are a number of examples:
*More than half of the population believes/think or etc. There are many who believe etc. We all agree on the etc. The majority of the vacant bother not etc.*

You can probably already see the pattern of this. If you are presented with such claims, you must always ask into the source. It is seldom existing. For far the most if those are  disingenuous.

I have just been together with a person who would spread his knowledge of our society. Such a person we should always listen to. There could be revealed very useful information.
All the time, he emphasized his "truths" with the words facts and fact. It should make his statement indisputable. When I drilled into his claims and asked for source references to his statements, then the gas went of the balloon. He only expressed his assumptions and his opinions.

There is nothing wrong with doing so. I do it myself all the time. I do it to be evaluated on my assumptions, opinions and theories, to see if thy sticks. Can they hold the water?
But that was not what he was doing. His "facts" didn't stand the distance.

He said in fact, that he was a tutor for children. It is probably true. But particularly tutorial he was in any case not. I expect that a tutor take the lead position with true guidance and useful, genuine information.
.

A special kind of claim-knowledge, calls upon us to be very much on guard. The case of surveys with commissioned result. They may be difficult to penetrate. Often they come from an analysis or research institute. The task initiator has simply ordered a quality-stamped argument for his point of view.

Hereinafter he may freely refer to the report as the simple truth.
This, there are several examples of in the past. **This is not a claim**, as you probably already know.
If such a report should be taken seriously, it is therefore a matter of planting pseudo knowledge, which is also a fraud..

# Genuine knowledge.

Genuine knowledge is exactly what we must strive to achieve And we shall have a lot of it. As many as possible in our society shall posses it. All our doubtful knowledge must be replaced by genuine knowledge. To achieve this will be a very long process. It can never be, and indeed nor shall it be finished.

We must, in every aspect stop the distribution of the many elements of false knowledge. Remember that all genuine knowledge derives from evidence.

We have a category of genuine knowledge, which not really can be explained. But it can always be proven. *Pythagoras theorem* is a good example of this. But there are many, many others, which I will not try to go into

# Faith (as in religious beliefs).

Faith is not knowledge  Nor does it pretend to be so. Faith is faith. Period. It requires no proofs at all. Faith belongs to the individual human being. You and me. It is in this connection quite peculiar, that a concept of state-religion exists.

Religion is purely based on faith. It has nothing to do with the state. Better said: It shouldn't have. There are, however much knowledge, which has started to be a faith in something. Faith assume thereby the nature of theory. When this theory then is sought to be proven, it could result in confirmed or ruled out knowledge. This is a way in which faith is working well in and with a Knowledge Society. Otherwise, as I said, it is just one of individuals many rights.

That faith is a opting of a point of view, which does not require evidence. Therein lies the whole value of a faith. You can say: "No matter what, then I believe"! All you believe in, is certainly of value to you.
A faith can provide relief for a pain. It is one of the powerful values of faith.
A faith can also give hope, where life otherwise seems heavy and hopeless. This is another strong valuable side of faith.

But the core in this matter is the fact, that faith is faith. It therefore has nothing to do with objective truth or genuine knowledge.

Try to taste this one: *We have religious freedom, but there is only one God from eternity to eternity?*

# "We shall have more..."

Or fewer, larger, smaller etc.

In the public domain, it is a widely used introduction of a sentence expressed by a politician. Of course there are many others, using this introduction. It is their solution. Almost on every issue, that needs a solution.

" We shall have more....."

Many times one must ask oneself: *Why?* And with good reasons. The issue, that is often referred to, as something we must have more of, is actually something, that didn't have the desired effect.
And for sure: the desired effect will not be produced by having more of it. It's that simple. Here is an example from my billiard universe. It's a statement from the chairman of a billiard club:

"We have now for five - no six years in a row, had an open-house-evening in the club. Prior to that evening, on a certain day, we placed a flyer under every wind screen cleaner on main road. If you can guess how many new members we got by that, so can I. Namely zero"!

Believe it or not: The intended to repeat the same open-house-evening again. In other words: More ineffective activities of the same kind. So my question is once again: *Why?*

Because the wanted to acquire more members. Yes – that is pretty obvious. And maybe an open-house-evening isn't a bad idea at all.

But something has to be done different. Let me at this point remind you of my personal motto: *Do as you use to do, and you will get the usual result!*

If you want a change, you have to do something different. Mark my words: I said *want* and not *wish.*

In the case with the billiard club, they could make a good use of a coach. A catalyst to promote and speed up good, appropriate amendments or changes to an open-house-evening. Proposal which resulted in plans, which was carried out. If these plans did not have the expected impact, they should continue with a new Coaching round. And so on till the expected effect occurred.

If the source of ideas ran dry, they would have to examine, whether the local geographical area could provide more members at all. But this is almost always the case.

We will therefore never get a Knowledge Society by establishing more schools, places at the universities, apprenticeships etc. Never.

We get it by **wanting** a change. Not more of the same inefficient stuff.

As I am writing this book, the public attention is drawn to the fact that the education at DJØF (a Danish higher education) is inadequate to finish with a passed examination. Yes – this is exactly what I'm talking about. The places for the education are there, but the quality of the education lacks to be competence giving. Isn't this a very simple problem? Isn't the solution equally simple? The Knowledge Society demands, that the education is elevated to a competence giving level!

This demand goes for all educations and all educational institutions of all kinds.

We have a business society, which requires more educated, competent staff. But the same business society requires not, within their own ranks, that there is the equivalent, required work placements to the completion of the ongoing education.

Does this make any sense at all? I, at least, cannot see it.
.

In relation to the subject of this book, I'll not go seriously into the ongoing debate about foreigners. But I would like to ask, whether it is in the interest of the Knowledge Society, that even highly educated people in our nowadays society, is running a taxi, cleaning offices, schools, hospitals etc.? All because we don't allow them to use their education in our country.
.

A large part of those people could immediately enter a qualified job in our country. With the already achieved education, skill and experience.

Some of them would require a light retraining or adaption to our local conditions. Most of them would need a basic education in our language. Not in order to co work with their colleagues, But to have a qualitative relation with people affected by their work.

Again –, it is not a simple issue with simple, already existing solutions?

I know it is. And I know it works.

We must have more people into work. Absolutely. No doubt about that. When we move a transfers income to a wage, then we will do more good things for society at the same time. We ease the pressure on the accounts, from where the transfer income is taken. At the same time we get more money for the state budget from the taxed wages. We give people a more meaningful life. We strengthen the peoples self-esteem. And much, much more.

But start the right place, with the right things.

Create the Knowledge Society which gives the vacant opportunity to take part in society as proud, respected members in our wonderful community.

"We must have more resources from the gray gold into the labour market"! Yes, of course. But there are far too many people, who tries to make themselves invisible, when they pass the age of 55. Because our working society far too often dumps these people. Solely due to their age. Or could it also be a parameter, that it is in this group we see the highest salaries due to seniority?

If this is the case, the solution is once again equally simple as is the problem. Adjust the raise of salary due to seniority. But make sure, that these adjustment rules are known in advance and in good time by the employee. He must have the opportunity to adjust his life and his private budgets to these rules in good time.

Or maybe our society should compensate partly or totally for these decreases in salaries? It is after all in everybody's interest, to have as many people as possible active in the working society for as long as possible. Not forced by duty, but by cheer lust.

I will not go on commenting on this subject. Luckily enough, we have the adequate number of experts, in this area. They must do their very best based on their knowledge.

And we must listen to them. But we shall do more the listening. We shall setup goals. We shall make planning, that support our goals. And we shall carry those plans out in life, with loyalty to the objectives.

# The internet

In a book on Knowledge Society one cannot bypass the Internet. I would therefore make some comments to it.

The invention of the Internet, is from my point of view one of the utmost innovations in the world. Entirely without precedence.

The Internet is both peacekeeping and a source of relaxation (détente) in the world. How is that? On the Internet anybody can get information on all and everything. Broadly. Many conflicts have arisen of ignorance and delusions of other countries and groups in different countries. On the Internet, you can learn about these foreigners without having to travel. Thus, you can get a more accurate and balanced picture of *foreigners*. Then they suddenly don't look so strange and different anymore. You also get a greater insight into the *aliens* own circumstances and problems. This understanding and insight gives you greater tolerance. Understanding and tolerance create peace and relaxation - détente.

*"On the Internet, one can also learn to produce bombs"!* Yes – and windmills and much more.

A used bomb is violence. The violence enters the scene, when the dialog cannot be established or quite simply stops. When the feeling of helplessness arises. When compromises are rejected. When insight and tolerance isn't present.

This is most often the reason for violence – but of course not always.

Strongest of all is the feeling of helplessness in relation to a reasonable demand for a change.

This feeling of helplessness is forced upon others, when ones own knowledge is either inadequate, or quite simply isn't used. Both are wrong. This is one of the many reasons, why we must have a Knowledge Society. In this we find knowledge, and it is used. In connection to this the Internet is a very powerful factor.

There is also a lot of false and misguiding "knowledge" on the Internet. It is thereby also used to spread misinformation. This can't be helped. But a strong Knowledge Society will recognise and reject such false knowledge.

Certain dictatorial States prohibit their citizens to use of the Internet. We are here dealing with States which knowingly misleads its own people. They sought kept misled and ignorant. Perhaps the human rights organizations could do something about this?

I will not in this book write more on Internet opportunities. I will simply point out that the positive aspects of the Internet, far outweighs the negative ones. The Internet is a part of the information society.

But so are books!

# Unused knowledge.

Unused knowledge, we obviously have a lot of. And for many reasons. We may have acquired the knowledge to use in a future situation, which never happens. Since both we and the World is constantly moving forward, we are regularly forced to revise our plans. That is how it is. And so it should be.

We may also acquire knowledge to deal with a crisis situation, which fortunately never happens. Thank you for that. But we are prepared, if the situation occurs.

These two examples of unused knowledge does not show bad sides of a Knowledge Society. On the contrary.

But I have a good example of unused knowledge, which is both negative, and actually quite stupid.

One of our major problems in our society is a widespread preponderance of too many people. A so-called fat-tax has just been pressed down on our society. Will it work? No. Fat-tax is an example of yet another whip, which we will get used to.

I myself, and presumably many others, have a problem with food on restaurants. There is too much of it in the individual portions. I lose appetite for food, when I am presented with these large portions. I also have to pay for the food.

I therefore often drops visits to a restaurant. I have chosen to eat, just till I'm full. No more. I therefore have to leave two-thirds or half of my food untouched. That I don't like. So – no thank you.

But many people feel that they must eat everything, they have paid for or which is put in front of them
This is quite understandable.

Many of us find the prices of food in a restaurant very high.

What knowledge based change does this call for?

Let's resume:
- Many people have far too high weight
- The served food is often far too much
- Visits to restaurants are rejected due to the size of the portions
- We eat all we are served
- Restaurant food is too expensive

The solution, I will propose, is that you can order a 50 % portion for a 60 % price. When I do not propose a 50 % price, it is because the work in the kitchen is almost the same as in a 100 % portion.

Try to see if we have not indeed addressed all the negative aspects, we know as knowledge, with a knowledge based solution?

It will, by the way, result in more visitors on the restaurants. More guests who find, that they could take their children with them too. Motivation for a dessert and a cup of coffee will also be greater. So the turnover will in any case not fall.

The restaurant, which is the first with a 50/60 % offer, will have a significant progress in number of guests. Satisfied guests.

Fat tax is not leading to an improved, better public health. It is a supplementary tax. So, for heaven's sake, call it what it is..

We are already today equipped with a great deal knowledge in many areas, which could result in positive, durable solutions, for the benefit of us all.

Get together and dig up your combined knowledge. Just think free of usual traditions in your own solutions. See how You will enrich yourselves and your society in this way.

*"Do as you use to do, and get what you used to get"!*

# We want the Knowledge Society!

At least somebody wants it. I want it. You probably want it too. And that is good.

But it is so far from enough to want the Knowledge Society. It requires a lot more than just wanting it. There is a need of some powerful locomotives to pull the heavy load in the right direction. The two far most powerful locomotives we have in our society are the politicians and the business society. It is at the same time totally impossible to achieve our goal without substantial financial resources.

Here we need the politicians to make some efficient decisions. Decisions based on knowledge about which measures will actually work for our purpose. Works. A very important key word and issue. Here faith and beliefs must take no active part. Only knowledge that works.

It is important to make it clear that such knowledge already exists. It's there. It is to be acquired where the need arises. It must be used. When the right decisions are taken, or as part of them, then appropriate appropriations must be given. For that we need the politicians. That is what they can do. That is what they must do.

Business society has several roles in the process. The first and leading role they have, is that of demanding knowledge. We must have a business society that persistently demands knowledge-strong competences. We have (also in Denmark) a business society that requires many different kinds of competences. This is very positive. It ensures, that when all these different competences are present and available, we will get all these competences, people, into the business society as active participants. The result will be a noticeable few idle hands. A relief of society's burdens. A happier society. And more proud people.

The next great role for business society, is that of the refining of its own resources through injection of new and updated knowledge. There must be constant focus on whether the individual resource is in possession of the necessary competences. All societies, ours no exception, is moving all the time. This demands constantly changes to new circumstances.

A competence can be obsolete. It must then either be ignored as historic or replaced by a modern, updated competence or knowledge.
A good example is the typewriter. A wonderful invention. Today it is virtually everywhere replaced by a PC and a printer. The same applies to the Slide Ruler and Erlangs Logarithm Tables (something Danish) and much else.

This means, therefore, that business must be a constant consumer of quality assured education and training courses.

We must also demand that the very large public sector follows the same guidelines as business. As citizens and business, we have requirements on a well-functioning, knowledge-based public sector.

When the public sector will get knowledge-based society characteristics and qualities, it will be a positive supporter of business. Not a deterrent. The individual citizen will also have a better and timely treatment.

But we must *want* the Knowledge Society, and not just wish that we will get it..

Our Knowledge Society also provides a very popular export product:
Competent people. Competent education. We will be able to offer a real, knowledge-based, highly competent educations to other countries.
Education which can be taken here in Denmark, or abroad led by Danes.

Yes – it is true: we must also obtain the best we can get both from abroad and abroad. We can not be self-sufficient in the best of all in our own country. But we can come closer to the State gradually and significantly.

That is what we need and want.

# My small history.

I have a very special background in order to deal with Knowledge Society. I know that the Knowledge Society is creating values. Not only to the individual, but just as much to society. I have seen a real added value in knowledge.

I have played billiard in approximately fifty years. The first forty-five years I learned virtually nothing. I sought not genuine learning. I *thought* that it came with time. Just as long as I played long enough and often enough. One day I realised, that it would never happen. I would never be more successful. It made me start thinking in new ways about the learning process..

My first constructive idea was, that there had to be a method to the attainment of knowledge and skills. The obvious to me was to look for such a method. I am talking here, especially of a method, a system, for learning the Danish game Five Pin Billiard (DK5PB for shortening).

It didn't exist. I was looking for a textbook, which contained a structured way to knowledge and skills. There were none. There was no signs that such a textbook ever would be written. I then got the idea, that I would write it myself.

Now – one cannot just sit down and write a textbook. It is an absolute demand to me that I *know* what I'm writing about. This put me in the process of a huge quantity of studies on the specific field, which is called DK5PB.

I started by tearing the whole game into atoms. I wanted to find and identify all details of the game. Then I put together related elements to manageable sizes. This I did for giving me the possibility to construct structured lessons.

I obtained in this way knowledge, that eventually became the base core in my educational system – the KBS model.

Then I took my own medicine. I wanted to see real proofs for my postulated ideas: That the knowledge I had achieved, could be converted into a competence. This was done through training of my knowledge into gained skills.

It actually worked - to my great joy. It was an absolutely, fantastic satisfaction to me.

My next step was so to convey my knowledge to others. I did so through my first Textbook *Pin Billiard – a crafts* (Keglebillard – et håndværk).
It was quite pioneering. There was for the first time a structured education system with guarantee of the effect

The pioneering was also that I made up with myths and the belief that if I just played long enough, then I would automatically be clever.

Pin billiard, as much else, can and must be learned systematically and structured. This Textbook was therefore a wakeup call to the existing practitioners of the game. One could also say that it was an appetiser.

When I had demonstrated the need and the impact of my system, I got the very obvious thought: How about making a complete apprenticeship for a pin billiard player?

This I have done. It is on the market (in Denmark) in the form of my most recent textbook *"An apprenticeship as Pin Billiard Player"* (En læreplads som keglebillardspiller).

My own club VBC - Vig Billiard Club - and DDBU – The Danish Billiard Federation – is active in the work of printing, marketing, sales and distribution. VBC has even reached a few modest but welcome sponsorships for publishing the book. I await with great interest the impact of a wide distribution of the book.

In a few general sections more, I will describe my education system – The KBS model – for you.

# Whip and carrot

Has this anything to do with Knowledge Society? Yes – and even very much so.

When we wish to direct our society in a certain, positive direction, it is the two methods used. Unfortunately, we almost exclusively use the whip. We are trying through punishment to have a positive change in behaviour and attitudes of the population. We say. But it does not work that way in a noticeable degree.

Efforts without effect, we have to abandon. I am often asking the question: "Does it work"? It is in this case most in concern of my calculations, my methods and my education. Yes – *they* works! All can by visual examination see it. It can, in other words, be proved. Only through that have they any value.

I cannot teach with a whipping. And I will not too. The carrot is in this case an added knowledge. Through the related training skills are added. Thereby a new competence is gained. This results in a significant progress in the game. That gives more success experiences. These causes personal joy and pleasure. And precisely that gives the eagerness to want more prosperity. This is also my own major motivation.

Where does society fail?

It is actually very simple to answer that question. The whip is used far too much. It really should not be used at all. Man is so by nature that he gradually become accustomed to the whip. To be punished. Only through addiction, he may survive mentally. This can, in particular, many earlier KZ-POW's confirm.

The whipping, most commonly used against society, is an economic one. A very widespread example is increasing the costs of certain products through increased taxes and charges. We make complaints of course of the increased expenditure and costs. But we get used gradually to the new conditions. That is why neither behaviour nor attitudes are changed.

Unfortunately, the fact is, that politicians often are operating with a hidden agenda. They want more money to finance the many, needed activities in our society. It is understandable. If only they would stop considering us as ignorant fools. They pay lip service in other words. Say as it is: **"We need to spend more money. That is why we penalize you who consume these products"!**

What are we, society and politicians to do instead of swinging the whip? We must use the carrot.

Populism waves all the time in our society. In shorter or longer periods individual items are on the carousel Yes – they may even have the tendency to go into self amplifying resonance. A good example of this is the existing hysteria around smokers. We are actually not far from the introduction of a yellow smoker-star worn externally on our clothes. Creates this certain associations? I suppose that it does?

Find and use the carrot instead. When the whip is the economy, the carrot must be that too. Set the price of tobacco to a normal value such as half of the current level. Give non-smokers reductions in the prices of a large number of the benefits. How about health related insurances etc.? The many user-paid surgeons are another suitable area. Spectacles and hearing aids can also be used.

Use our society's many experts to find all the appropriate areas which might favour non-smokers economically. That will work. It can be seen in a each supermarket, and any other outlet, which operates with periodic or permanent discounts.

One of our society's and populisms many favourite horses to ride, is the public's consumption of alcohol. Forget about punishing consumers of spirits through high sales prices. Use the carrot. Set the price of all beverages with an alcoholic strength less than 3 percent drastically reduced. Remove all taxes and state charges from this group of beverages. When it comes to choosing a beer, it seems ridiculous, that a non-alcoholic beer costs a lot more than an ordinary lager.

Make it attractive to purchase the alcohol weak or non-alcoholic beverages. It is working. It will also create greater confidence in our politicians, when we can see that things are linked. As it is now, it is too easy to see through the hypocrisy in the statements saying, that we must reduce or stop alcoholism.

I have briefly mentioned smoking and alcohol. The model can be used on all issues, where a positive change of attitudes and behaviour being sought implemented.

I was about to write *"is desirable"*. However, **there must never be operated with a desire but a will.** Desire is linked with faith. Faith is not knowledge. In a Knowledge Society we are taking our decisions on the basis of knowledge.

In that way are the carrot and the whip linked together with a Knowledge Society.

# The puppy.

I have recently acquired me yet another dog. A puppy. It's a Cairn terrier. She is both sweet and wise. I also think that she is beautiful. I really must admit that I love my dog. But she is also full of with. Just as she should be.

I want, however, that the dog grows up to be a good and loving mate. I want also, that it does the right things. I wouldn't have it doing all the wrong things. This requires a good education. That I am 100 % prepared to give her.

I am right now in full activity to give my dog a puppy-education. It does not work, if I at the moment are trying to give it a education as an adult dog. We do not let a 7-year-old start in secondary school.

My Puppy has already in 2 – 3 weeks time learned many things. For the benefit and pleasure of both the dog and me. The process of change is here exactly a change in attitudes and behaviour as I referred to earlier. A change of attitudes from both the dog and me. Yes – I must also have a change in attitudes.

When I want a good and loving dog, I must give it a good and loving upbringing.

When we want to have a Knowledge Society, then we must also have the change into a behaviour, which creates and maintains Knowledge Society.

With my puppy it's actually quite simple. I must reward and praise everything that my puppy does right. And I mean *everything*. I should not punish the puppy for what it does wrong. I have only to point out, friendly and clearly, that I will not accept this behaviour. If , what the puppy does is wrong, but not harmful, I ignore it. It is education, which works. It has already given great results.

Another thing that works is that both my wife and I totally agree about the puppy's upbringing. This creates consistency. We act and react in the same way towards the puppy, in what upbringing concerns. This generates meaningful consistency. It feels god to the puppy. And it generates the desired results in a pleasant way. At the same time we give individual loving care.

I know that when I later on is building based on this good upbringing of the puppy, I'll get a wonderful adult dog. A dog adapted to the good life, it must have. And the dog will have some good and affectionate people, which is adapted precisely this dog.

My dog has a hunger for learning. It is accustomed to this: What it learns from us will be rewarded.

My dogs name is Freja. She is a full term family member. She has her own rights and obligations. We show her respect and she does the same for us (most of the time).

Now – why am I telling you about my puppy? Because the above described situations are an exact micro cosmos, on what we want to happen, when we want a Knowledge Society.

I will ask of you to use your great ability for abstraction, as the intelligent person you are. Here you have one of your great competences. With the dog in mind: Look at the initial face and the method. Look at the results. Look at the used resources. Try to turn all of these elements for a situation, where we initiates a Knowledge Society. Do you see the similarities?

Imagine that we by now have initiated a sustainable Knowledge Society. We have a sound basis to build on. We must continue building through to make the Knowledge Society self-generating and self-supplying.

A society where acquired knowledge creates desire for more knowledge. _Because_ we have obtained knowledge. We must work in four general directions:

- We must find _new_ knowledge.
- We must acquire _existing_ knowledge
- We must disseminate _already acquired_ the knowledge
- We must _use_ our knowledge

You must also know, that I know, that even though my methods are simple, and indeed even the fact that they works, it should not obscure the fact, that a lot of work lies ahead of us.

The benefit of the effort, that we must make, is that it will be more and more easy as we go along. We will simply be better equipped to do the task and solve the problems.

That's the way the Knowledge Society works.

No magic, just knowledge and work.

# Curiosity and knowledge-hunger.

Once again the computers vocabulary had to be extended. We probably need many more, useful words in our language. Not weird words, but useful words.

The Danish word for curious is a combined word. The two words *news* and *stingy* are put together. The latter has a negative sound to it. But put together, they form a very positive word.

A large part of the evolution of mankind is in fact created through curiosity. It is therefore due to serious criticism, when displayed curiosity is either neglected or shown of as bad behaviour. Particularly when concerning children's curiosity. It is incompetent adult behaviour. A person unable or unwilling to answer a child's many questions. A question is an expressed motivated desire of gaining knowledge. It must never be neglected.

All sides of our society must encourage and motivate inclination of asking questions. Of course we can reject certain questions. For example, the questions of personalities, which we will not share with others, like knowledge on certain aspects of our personality. It may also concern on knowledge, which will be harmful to the specific time, if it is published. But in general, we must respond to all the questions.

*What*? And *how*? These two fundamental questions are very important, They initiates injection of knowledge. They are bound together with the third important questioning word: **Why**?

*What* and *how* must be linked with the logical explanation through *why*. Only thus can injected knowledge be stored in the consciousness as meaningful knowledge. Knowledge that makes sense.

So much on curious. What about knowledge-hunger? Where will that enter the stage?

When I speak of hunger, no distinction is made between genuine hunger and titbit-hunger. They share many characteristics. We are all in a position to feel titbit-hunger to the positive, healthy things. Not only on the unhealthy. Hunger translates into needs and aspirations. If it is possible, we will cover our needs and aspirations. Without the moral finger on the excessive consumption, this is both right and healthy.

To create and maintain, not to talk of the further development of a Knowledge Society, there must be a latent knowledge-hunger present in the individual. It is an absolute necessity. That is why this hunger for knowledge must be encouraged, nursed and satisfied..

I will not give specific practices in order to stimulate knowledge-hunger. I would just draw to your attention the great importance of the carrot in this context too.

Make it attractive to acquire knowledge. Make sure that the acquired, trained knowledge trigger rewards. It can be done in many ways. Cupboard a symposium, where various experts can make bets with their own knowledge and experience in terms of rewarding carrots..

Consider what you will carry out. And do it! Intentions have no value in this context. Promises and wishes are just as inapplicable. Only concrete plans, carried out, have value. It starts with *I will*.

So there is a major task for all parts of our society to encourage, stimulate and satisfy the knowledge-hunger.

It is not all to come from the State or the community. Much can, and indeed shall come from the individual companies and institutions.

It must also come from caring, responsible parents. I have a small, simplified model over some of the places where knowledge-hunger should be encouraged. It is at the same time the model of the places, where the knowledge-hunger must be met and satisfied..

.

| Play school | Pre school | Private schools | University | Apprenticeship |
|---|---|---|---|---|
| Kindergarten | Primary school | High | Higher preparation | Academy |

| **The home** |
|---|

(My knowledge of other countries various institutions are, as you can see, rather limited. And the list in far from being complete.)

It will be clear to everyone that it is quite impossible for a single person to complete such a model. Here, all parts of our society must give their contribution. In all places where people meet, can knowledge-hunger be tickled. On a closer inspection, you see that just knowledge-hunger is one of the foundations, on which we must build a Knowledge Society.

Almost any kind of durable changes in our society regarding attitudes and behaviour starts at home. In the first part of our lifetime, home is also our comfortable frame of reference.

Here we are gently led into the right direction. Here we are allowed moderate misbehaviour, in search of the necessary borderlines to be found.

Here we achieve loving and timely care in the context of our *formation*. Here absorb we our first knowledge.

Therefore, we must also give *home* knowledge on how we as parents/Guardians prepares the formation of the Knowledge Society from the bottom of the individual child, ***which is a human being.***

Try to elaborate further on the aphorism hunger/knowledge-hunger. There are many similarities. We eat, when we are hungry. We don't eat, when we are satisfied. Having eaten, some time has to pass, before we will be hungry again. We can be titbit-hungry, although we are satisfied. We eat normally not something that isn't appetizing-. The more appetizing the food looks and smells, the more we are prepared to eat etc.

We have a major challenge in presenting the offering of knowledge supply in an appetizing manner. It is necessary, but not enough, that the offering of knowledge supply is present. Take part actively in finding the lifeblood – the nerve - to more knowledge in the individual. Here you are allowed to lure. However, it requires a certain degree of, selective moderation. Are we offered too much food in a time, we can either not decide what we want, or we will lose simply the appetite.

# The KBS model

This is primarily my recipe, as to how a person can be a highly skilled billiard player.
If this was the sole possible usage of the KBS model, I would never have written this book.
But this is far from the fact.

When one wish to build up a competence, some quite specific foundation stones are required. Fortunately they are quite few in numbers. And they are not difficult to understand. In these facts lies a part of their value. I always strive for simplicity in my solutions, even to rather complex problem situations.

When we talk Knowledge Society, my starting point is always the individual.
We will never go further, if we do not pay respect to the individual. The best of it is, that it does not impede the transformation process. The process that takes us from where we are, to where we want to be. Isn't this good? Or does it have the sounds of utopia?

The opposite would be, that we dealt with people in blocks. We have done so for generations. The result, we can see everywhere around us: Lost people. Semi- or insufficient educated people. Uncertainty. Competencies, which does not keep par value.

When one wishes to make some good sausage meat, one takes some good meat and chops it properly and homogeneous. Then you have a good sausage meat. A base sausage meat – for sure. But still sausage meat.

The same meat could be dealt with quite different – individually – with some marvellous, culinary experiences to follow.

Let us get back on the ground. Let us look at the foundation stones to be, in order to build a Knowledge Society. This is, of course, what we want to do.

The Knowledge Society is a large, complex organism. No individual needs to embrace or comprehend all of it. It is in the final instance built up by competences within individuals – people. It is, therefore the individuals education and training, we must focus on. But it has to be *real educations,* which results in a competence growth.

It all begins with a need, I called it knowledge hunger, a will to achieve a competence. If the need isn't real, the education and training will not result in a competence. If not the desire to a competence is present, then the education and training is wasted.

The keyword here is motivation. It can never be fertilized too much. This goes for the busyness society, the public sector and the education sector as wel ass for the individual.

Hence we anticipates, that a person initially when entering an education, is in fact motivated.

Now we proceed to the KBS model.

# The short version

It sometimes can be both pleasant and convenient to view a system in form of a diagram.

It may also be useful to see a system as interrelated, connected blocks.

So – here are a very few blocks, that illustrates the KBS model:

(The blueprint of the model is so vitally important, that I'll give it a page of its own).

The KBS model diagram

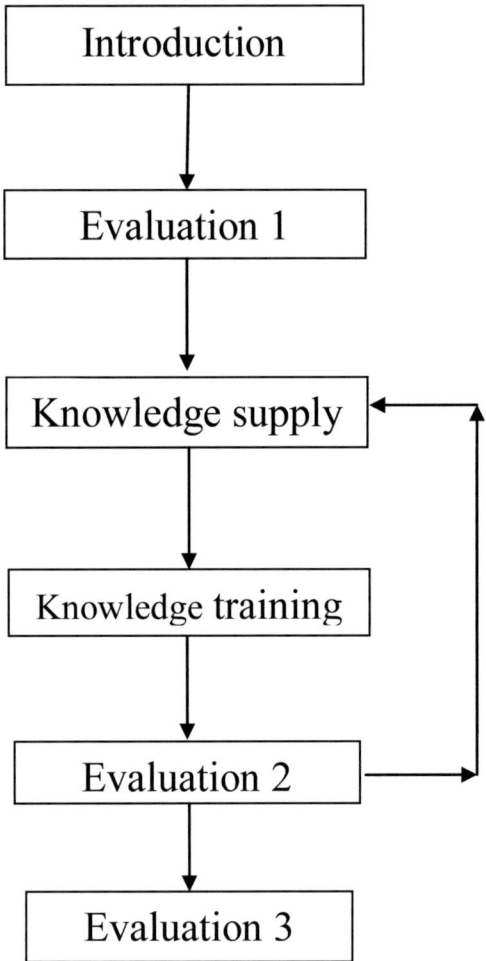

The hereby outlined model looks at least very simple.

Does this look like *The Emperor's new clothes?* I can give you the guarantee, this is not the case.

But of course, it cannot stand alone. So now I'll give you an explanation on the individual modules.

# Introduction

This is the welcome-package to an education or a framework process.
Its main purpose is to make the pupil ready to start an education.
We must equip the pupil properly, for the work he must carry out. (I use in general the designations *pupil* and *he* regardless of nature of the training or the gender).

The introduction may be quite extensive depending on the nature of, and the education itself. It can and must, in other cases, be very brief. This may, for example be illustrated by a persons start in a nursery school or the start of a university degree. But in both cases there is a need for and requirements of an introduction. The – Kindergarten and nursery school are also places for education and training.

- **The competence**    What have the pupil gained after the education? Here we must clearly state, what the pupil have learned, when the education and training period is completed. I have here quite clearly to point out that we are talking about **what the pupils have learned**, not only heard of. It is therefore a site promise to the forthcoming pupil. The site must be kept up for the commitment. It is a knowledge-based society demand.

- **Time**                  When is the education to take place? Pupils must be fully informed of the educations time aspects. They should be informed of the days on which education takes place. When are the individual lessons? How long are the lessons? Pupils must be well clothed to meet well-prepared to all teaching. Where the knowledge-training is outside the time for lessons, when is it the then to take place and where? Is the training homework? What of holidays and education free days? No pupil must feel uncertain about the time aspects of the education, when the introduction is given

- **Equipment**        What is the pupil expected to possess, when the education starts? It may be purely material things as the equipment and utensils, clothing etc. There may also be a matter of the acquisition of prior, called for competences. When the pupil starts on the education, he must be lacking nothing, that makes it difficult or directly hampers a successful education.
- **Customs**        Which rules of conduct is applicable? How does locality hierarchy look and work? There should be informed of a possibly canteen or other eventual food-arrangements? How about accommodation? Are there transport offering/choices? This is, on everything that happens outside the education. I therefore cannot make this list complete for all circumstances. The task falls on the individual education sites.

At the individual education sites, this list must be tailored to match exactly this site. But the introduction must be there. As much as possible must be accompanied in the form of written material. This is to support the students memory. He must already through the introduction have acquired valuable, relevant knowledge. Knowledge is what he expects. Knowledge is what we promise him. Knowledge is what we will give to him.

After the introduction the pupil are also able to inform his network on the actual, future relationships and conditions.

The introduction will often be divided into two parts: The introduction before and at the first appearance. The part, which is before the first appearance, shall be made available in due time, that pupils in his own pace may make himself familiar with the material. Perhaps there has to be additional materials for a third party?

# Evaluation 1

This is a pre-evaluation on the individual pupil. It has to be taken prior to the education.
The evaluation must be summary, covering the immediately following block of education.

The purpose of this evaluation is to probe for the pupils pre-knowledge and skills in the following, coming subject(s). It will, at the same time, clearly show the pupils strengths and weaknesses in relation to these subject(s). It is however not a thorough GAP analyzes. But it will make the teacher able to give individualized education.

It must never be assumed that everybody in the education group is equally aware or ignorant. We are clearly forced to get rid of block-teaching. Not as the starting point, but as the essential method. We must always think in terms of teaching individuals. That is why Evaluation 1 is so important.

In many cases may Evaluation 1 be executed in good time, before the education starts.
It will, as I mentioned earlier, give the teachers opportunity for a prior information. It will facilitate his preparations for the future team (which may be 1 pupil).

It is important to point out that Evaluation 1 is not expected to demonstrate great knowledge of the forthcoming issue(s), if any at all. As important as it is, it must not be presented in a stress-giving form. It cannot disclose an unexpected incompetence. Incompetence is precisely our starting point for an education.

Evaluation 1 is an obvious tool in recruitment of a person for particular job. An appointment however, should not be conditional on the outcome of an Evaluation 1.

Imagine which valuable tool it is for supplementing of the existing competences.

The catch about it is, that *you* must develop Evaluation 1. Or is it not on the other hand, a great advantage to have made oneself quite clear, of the demands there are to the job in question?

# Knowledge supply

This is most often referred to as educating or teaching. There are numerous variants of types of teaching. Not all fit equally well to the various subjects.

Education at the detail level should primarily be made on the, for the issue and the pupil(s), most appropriate form. It is the starting point.

There will almost always be some difference in the individual's best learning method. It will therefore be useful to get the individual pupils to realize his best method or form of learning. To make him aware of this. Many have never really thought about the method which suits them best. Here, much can be gained.

As a teacher, it is also important to have knowledge of this side of the individuality. It will be the best impetus to find the most appropriate teaching method in relation to the subject and individual. It will also remove some sources of irritation.

When the pupil is aware of his best method of perception (learning), the teacher will be asked some repeated forms of questions:

- Couldn't you just tell me ... ?
- Couldn't you just show me ... ?
- Can I just see ... ?
- Can't I just try myself to ... ?
- Couldn't I just try to read it myself?
- Etc..

All these issues are not attempt to disrupt or delay education. They are a clear expression of the students insight into his own situation around his education. When the teacher is aware of this, then education can easily be adjusted to cover the needs of the most of students.

It will avoid many of the questions. Removing them entirely is difficult. It is also not the intention. The questions too are an expression of commitment.

Never make a block of teaching greater than that you can come all around on the subject. You have to make sure, that there is enough time for rounding up the issue without haste. Set time for questions. Set some time for unforeseen disturbances.

It may seem as if, there will be very little time for the real education or teaching. This however, is not the case. The time spent on real education, must be characterised by quality. It is a demand from the Knowledge Society. You thereby teach more in less time.

As a teacher, you must always be well-prepared and in good time. You have to be sure that everything needed for the teaching, is present. That everything works properly.

The same, you *must* require of your pupils.

I will go into the education issue in more details later on.

# Knowledge training

This is of far greater importance, than most people know or is aware of. But it is a very important component of the KBS model. And why is that?

***The most important reason is, that you can only store your knowledge thoroughly through training.***

It is training that does the work of encasing the newly acquired knowledge within you. It is training, which gives you an ability to use your knowledge. Training gives you competence. Training gives you security. Knowledge plus training creates the Knowledge Society.

Training must be set up and arranged in such a way, that pupils learn to look at, examine, and interpret these exercise tasks from different angles. There must be variance in task formulation in.n.t. the straight road to the use of the newly acquired knowledge. The task may by all means complicate the solution. The education must however have a quality and variance, that all tasks can be solved by using the newly acquired knowledge (and even earlier acquired knowledge). ***This is a demand.***

There is another reason for you to train your newly acquired knowledge. Trained knowledge is like a tool in your "toolbox". When you facing a task, you can only use the available tools - those you possess. You are in other words to train what you will use. For you use only what you have trained. It is that simple.

.

Ergo: When you, as a teacher, build up training programs for your pupils (I use the term Game Plan on training program), so please try to ensure diversity.

Give the pupils an opportunity to train the new knowledge from diversity in these tasks nature. This will give the pupils the option to analyze a problem, and then chose and use the right tools for the solution.

Too often we see that people cannot solve simple tasks, because they do not look like business as usual. I will later on use a little time on problem analyzes.

Game Plans should include the new knowledge's entire curriculum. It is a part of the guarantee, which we gave the pupils. He would have learned, what he was taught. The ultimate requirement from the Knowledge Society is: Only genuine competences counts.

A later section will be devoted to Game Plans.

# Evaluation 2

Following the completion of learning and training, it is time for an evaluation.

We must now see to what extend each and every student has learned the new substance. None of my evaluations of the KBS model has the character of examination. Examinations are not at all part of the KBS model. So it is, because they have no value at all, in a Knowledge Society. Period. Or was this a little too easy to claim?

Yes I suppose it was. An examination, as we know it today, results in an examination degree, a letter or a digit. In Denmark it's called a character. Its nature is of later to be used as a parameter in many situations. It is not a true expression of the individual's knowledge and skills. It only shows what the individual could provide in the given situation under the given circumstances.

It reflects not a possible stress-effect for example. There may be very many good reasons that the individual didn't performed at his best during an examination. Reasons, which an examination cannot respect. The student cannot use the examination result for *a future purpose*. It is just a definitive number, which is harping on his back.

This must therefore be replaced by evaluations. They have great values in the development of a Knowledge Society. And they *do* have a purpose for the future.

An evaluation 2 has the following characteristics:
It deals with all of the latest, learned subject. There will be a few, representative tasks. Task results must be convertible into figures. It must not be characterised by pressure of time.

The entirely new epoch-making difference on examination and evaluation is that the evaluation at the same time is *a genuine GAP analysis*.
.
It will clearly show, which part of the substance is learned sufficiently to the level of a skill or a competence. This is one of the great values of the KBS model. GAP's should be closed. GAP'S will be closed. Was this not done, we could not give an education guarantee. ***But this we shall do. And this we will do.*** This too is a requirement of the Knowledge Society.

Education must therefore include catching up the inadequate knowledge and skills of the individual. This can be done in several ways without injury or slow down on the ongoing education.

Evaluation 2 shows when, and to what extent, we can continue with new learning. We don't continue by building upon clay. This is very important too.

# Evaluation 3

Here is the KBS model's successor of the inapplicable examinations.

Evaluation 3 contains all the substance, as the total education has covered. Not necessarily 100 %. But to a degree that clearly shows, whether the pupil has received the full benefits of the educational curricula. To see whether the promised and expected competences is achieved.

My experience collected through my long business life shows, that the most graduations  or ending examination's leaves out large substance areas from the first parts of the education. This means, that such an examination does not guarantee the true value of the early skills acquired.

This is very open to criticism. An education must contain the substance or the competences that is expected to be used after training. It must therefore be ensured that all the substance is stuck as knowledge, skills and thus competences.

The result of an Evaluation 3 is either *passed* or *not passed*. Whether the student has passed or not, is determined by a percentage of true answers in the test. The individual education, sets the level of the required percentage..

My education in billiard calls for example for a minimum of 75 %. Other educations would be likely to require 80 % or 90 %. Very few should, however require 100 %.

When deciding the individual percentage values, my guidelines of procedure are these:

- Education aiming at, or leading to a job, requires a substantially higher percentage value than educations taken for usage in leisure time, hobbies etc.
- Competences that require *at hand* knowledge requires a higher percentage value than competences that allows time for a look-up.
- Competences used in field operations in for instance remote, isolated areas requires too a high percentage value. You're on your own.

Do you see my point? Do you see a common denominator in the above? If so – you are likely well qualified to set the percentage value for the Evaluation 3 on educations where you have the responsibility.

However, it is not so, that because a pupil has not passed, he is blank on the incorrect or incomplete answers. Through the use of the KBS model there will most often be rather small GAP's in knowledge or knowledge training.

Like Evaluation 2, Evaluation 3 is too a GAP analysis. Here it is however an exposure of the GAP's in the overall knowledge and skills. Note that I use the term *knowledge and skill*. It is precisely this combination, which constitute a competence.

# The navigation chart

*" It is one thing to understand a navigation chart, another to be in command of a vessel"!*

A Knowledge Society also demands something else fundamentally different and new: We must on all educations be allowed to carry out an Evaluation 3 again. Indeed several times, if there is a need and desire for it.

It is far more important for the Knowledge Society, that more will have their for example Baccalaureate or any other approved conclusion of an education scheme.

Knowledge Society needs very many people, which has passed. Only then, we have contributed to our society knowledge in the form of competences.

Each attempt on an evaluation 3 must be complete. It must not include only the holes found on a previous evaluation 3. The student, whom we return to our society after a passed evaluation 3, must be completely equipped to use his new skills acquired. It is our promised guarantee, which we thus fulfil.

It was a review of the KBS model. It shows the necessary funds to the attainment of a Knowledge Society.

Maybe it's too simple in your opinion.. But it is precisely my clear objectives: To create simple solutions to complex problems. Solutions which are relatively simple to implement. Solutions that works.

My KBS model will inevitably be meeting many opponents or negative critics. It cannot be avoided in a society where we are used to complex solutions on the relatively simple problems for decades. Yes indeed for centuries.

Many would certainly in veiled pleasure eagerly plead for the Janteloven (a Danish issue explained below*). Unfortunately, this is seen far too often. But I welcome any attempt to overrule the true values of the KBS model. But only if they are based in proved arguments – is genuine knowledge. In this case, the KBS model should be improved. But it must not be made more complicated or complex.

I will now go on to explain some important ingredients in preparation of the society to the future Knowledge Society.

*) *Janteloven*
It is not a true law, but mere a number of bad opinions on other people. They were gathered and written down by the Danish author Axel Sandemose quite many years ago in his novel "A refugee crosses his tracks":

## The Law of Jante
- You shall not think that you are special
- You shall not think that you are of the same standard as us
- You shall not think that you are wiser than us
- Don't fancy yourself as being better than us
- You shall not think that you know more than us
- You shall not think that you are more (important) than us
- You shall not think that you are good at anything
- You shall not laugh at us
- You shall not think that anyone cares of you
- You shall not think that you can teach us anything

# Appendix contents

In the appendix I will later on describe a Knowledge Society based education.
It means in this case a large amount of the substance of billiard.

My aim with this is to show the high demands for educational quality. You must therefore only regard it as my example of a program of educational framework, which can be used widely in almost any kind of education.

You can read it now, if you want to. You can also wait, and read it at the end of the general part of the book.
.
If you yourself plays billiard, you may actually learn a lot about this game by examining the content more meticulous.

Have you absolutely no interest in billiard, should you yet inspect the substance to learn more about my elections of structure, my method and my quality assurance.

We are jumping rapidly further along.

## Enough on billiard

Quite clearly that it was a huge bite of technique around DK5PB.. Please disregard from the billiard technical issue and look at the framework displayed..

I only have shown the example of training day one. I wish to use this only in order to show the tight methodology. It felt in no way prohibitive or restrictive, when I followed the method in practice. On the contrary, it was a pleasant structure to support myself during the work.

I had put in short breaks of about 5 minutes between each part session. It gave the necessary breath of air and distance between the individual exercises. Your brain should be refreshed between shifts in subjects.

But where was the Knowledge Society, in all the talk about billiard?

In order to establish an effective process of change, I first needed to provide me a wealth of knowledge on education with new methods.

Through quantities of trials, calculations and checks made I clear keen rules on how the individual types of dessin's had to be played (dessin equals ball setup + solution). These were enshrined in clear, simple tables. This was at the same time both obtaining and verification of new knowledge.

I trained my new knowledge on education through the use of the KBS model.

I trained my knowledge on standard dessin's through following my keen tables inlaid in my Game Plans. (Now the term Game Plan probably makes more sense).

I had relatively quickly proof of a clear progress on all the areas concerned. Not a perceived progress, but a direct measurable prosperity.

Once again:

*Remove billiard from my examples. Insert rather any other area, where a knowledge-based process of change is needed. Follow the model and see that it works.*

Experience the delight in appropriately, rationally to acquire both knowledge and skills – and thereby competences.

As teacher, instructor, or coach you must also see joy to disseminate correct knowledge, which is trained by your pupils to new competences.

You must also know, feel and recognize that nothing will come of itself. The KBS model is the structure and method, to be followed. The content, you yourself have the responsibility to find and put into the model.

Now, I've played enough on the lyric harp. We must press on with some substance.

# SMART goal

To work towards an objective, a goal, is not strange for the most of us. Fortunately, this is at the same time very attractive to work toward a goal.

In fact, any process of work should have a goal ahead and attached of it. To achieve the goal is a wonderful experience of success, which creates pleasure. Pleasure in the individual and in larger or smaller groups.

This feeling of satisfaction is so important, because it is fertile ground for optimism and renewed desire to achieve new goals.

Children realize early the need to have a goal. Give some children a ball and an area. Some of the first they do is to establish a goal. It is causing more value to them playing toward a goal. Just kicking or throwing around with a ball will soon become quite boring.

Imagine you to be put a shovel in hand with information on digging, until someone say stop. Or dig for five hours. It just doesn't work. It seems immediately far more motivating, if you have to dig, to a specific target is reached.

The goal is therefore important. That is why it is also important that there are quality in the definition of goals. On this, I'll dedicate the next few pages.

That a goal is SMART, is not my own invention. There are also several interpretations of the concept SMART goals. This is mine then, or at least the one I've chosen:

- **S**   Specifically
- **M**   Measureable
- **A**   Attractive
- **R**   Realistic
- **T**   Time-definite

These is clear ultimatums to all goals properties.

You cannot define a goal, when starting with statements such as these:

- I wish .....
- I would like to think that .....
- It would be nice if .....
- Etc.

Will of change is required to define usable goals. Therefore the definition of a goal starts with: *"I will ... "*

## Specifically

That a goal must be specific, is the first, important quality. Never: more than, more, a little bit more, something more etc.

- If it was the desire to loose weight, the goal could be: I will weigh 80 kilograms. Not less than today, but 80 kilograms.

- I will investigate whether there is a link between cadmium and arthritis amongst silversmiths in Denmark.

- I will get our team up into 2. division next year.

## Measureable

The above-mentioned 8O kilo's are directly measurable and therefore an appropriate a goal.

The Cadmium-arthritis study is made measureable by indicating a study of 1200 silversmiths from 150 firms.

2. Division is also a clear goal, as it is easy to see whether it is acquired or not.

Perhaps there has to be produced 2,540,000 copies of something. It is, of course a very clear goal. A large goal perhaps, but it is in any case very precise and measureable.

## Attractive

This is all about motivation. You are in other words to make it quite clear to yourself, why you want to achieve the goal you set up.
.

- I want to weigh 80 kilos, because this will make me think better of myself. It will increase my self-esteem and self-respect.

- I will produce 2,540,000 elements, because I thereby is linking company BlaBla closer to my own firm. Doing so I'll have increased the likelihood for future demands on several products.

- I will bring our team up in the second division, because I thereby can achieve more sponsor contracts. This gives me the possibility to do more for all my players and not only for the few selected ones.

You need a quite clear good reason for yourself, to take on a task.
The task can be quite tedious.
The task may be due for substantially log time.

*You get the courage and endurance through your own motivation.*

## Realistic

I am speaking here on a clear, objective assessment of the current situation.

The required resources must also be taken into account.

The timescale has here a key value.

You are most welcome to setup high goals. However, they must be achievable – and thereby realistic.

If your goal is very high – defined as the distance between your current level and the level you want to reach – you may have great advantage in breaking down your final goal into part goals. This enables experiences of success throughout the entire process.

The demand for quality in defining part goals matches the demands for the end goal.

## Time definite

Some deadlines may be given in advance

- It will often be so, in the case of a supply to a customer. It could be useful to define some small quantities with corresponding shorter deadlines. This will give you more options for adjusting the production on eventually, discovered early lacks.

- A concept such as before the winter 2013-2014 may, for example be clarified as November the first 2013.

- With regard to a loss of weight, it must be *possible* for you to lose the necessary number of kilograms **with the effort you will make**.

- You want your team in the second division at the start of season 2014-2015. This time limit is each year a specified date.

- The result of your cadmium-arthritis study you will be presented at May the first 2015.

Should you have achieved your goal within the established sessions time limit, then you have the possibility of redefining your goal to be higher.

You can also choose to give yourself a breathing space before you define your next goal.

Or this could be the time, where you choose to do some of the activities, you may have had to set aside in order to achieve your goal.

I have explained my views on SMART goals. I am convinced that you can see it usefulness in making your goals SMART GOALS.

*Do not compromise in the quality of your goal-definitions.*

# Coaching

In connection to the subject of the billiard club, I mentioned the concept *Coaching.*

I am aware of the fact, that there are real educations within the Coaching. These are important too. I am talking prejudice here for something much simpler. Coaching in the everyday life.

*My* coach is a catalyst in everyday life. A valuable partner in at least two situations. The first is, when there is a problem, which requires a solution, but the way of approaching the problem is not obvious.
The other is, when there is a will of change, but the approach and procedures to be taken is unclear.

In both cases, the sufficient knowledge is often already present. It must simply be helped forward into light. Here is Coaching of great help.

As a coach you will use a number of W-words. What, where, why, who, when, plus the how etc.

Coaching helps in other words to a clear, facts based problem definition. Once the problem definition is clear and understood, the solution often comes out of the dim quite easily.

This is the starting point of change procedure. You should know what you are faced with, the situation which you are in, what you have available of resources, etc.

Then the coach helps you to define one or more SMART goals, which, accompanied by a suitable solution, will solve the problem.

He will guide you in making *your own*, durable planning and solution.

The entire problem definition is however your own. So is the solution proposal. But most importantly of all is: The planning is your own.
You will thereby have the very best kick off with a high degree of both motivation and commitment.

In the end of the coaching you go through it all. See, whether your planning an your solution encompasses the entire problem. See, if you are comfortable with your solution. Revise the planning, if so needed.

## *And then work your plan.*

A good coach will always seek pre-knowledge about your work. This is to make him more qualified in asking into the core of your problem or your process of change decision.

It will not be unusual for the coach to come up with proposals. But it will always be in question form: Can we do this? Is it possible to --? What happens if --? What if not --?

You are the expert on your own territory. This expertise is respected by the coach, and he will help you to use it.

Can you, from what I have said see, that there not always will be a need for an external coach? That there quite often within your own ranks already are people, who are qualified to carry out the Coaching in certain areas?

That you yourself in fact could take the role as the coach in many situations? That you actually can be your own coach from time to time?

If you want to make more use of in-house Coaching, I would strongly recommend you to provide you more knowledge of coaching, than what I have given you

It can, of course have great benefits to include a third person as coach in many situations. Fresh eyes without preconceived ideas. It is an old, known Council. And it is forever true.

So much on coaching in this instance. Now, we will look at one of my own invented tools from the KBS model *Cocoaching.*

# Co-coaching

It sounds perhaps a little, as if I was a stammer. However, this is not the case. But I would like to look a little more closely on this word-Bastard.

One of the things we have done wrong for generations, is to have one teacher to disseminate the knowledge to a group. As the starting point, there is nothing wrong with that. It just doesn't work in the long run. This we can observe as a knowledge in wide education communities around us. What is wrong?

The teacher is a human being with the knowledge and competence, he is in possession of. He has his own personal characteristics. These include sympathies and antipathies. He has his personal attitudes and his own commitment to the learning substance. So it must be necessarily.

The group, he is about to teach, consists of equally many individualists like as himself. Here lies the problem.

If we could say that all members of the group was just equally intelligent and motivated, we were indeed very lucky. This however, is never the case. And many thanks for that. But this diversity makes some specific demands to the education framework. Demands, that can be quite difficult to honour.

Another important reason, as to why traditional group or class teaching is not functioning, is diversity in perception capabilities. The method, in which the individual prefers to be given new knowledge.

You will rarely see students, with only one strong method of perception. Most of the students will have two or three strong methods of perception.

A class or a group can presumably often be divided into smaller groups with almost identical perception forces. And then there will be some outsiders.

The traditional way of *"One class – one teacher"* cannot handle this. It's natural, but useless anyway.

*Provided, that we want the Knowledge Society!*

If this constellation of problems should be solved, it would require more teachers for one session of education. Such resources we will rarely have at hand.

**But this is also not necessary. We could make use of** *co-coaches.*

Roughly we could operate with the division of a class into some minor groups:

| Jetset |
|---|

| Craftsmen |
|---|

| Truckers |
|---|

| Trailers |
|---|

This is, of course some quite foolish names, so let us call them: Grp1, 2, 3 and 4

**Grp1** Will immediately have acquired the substance at the teacher presentation and walkthrough. They probably have a good range of strong perception forms.

**Grp2** Will have acquired the most of the substance of the primary presentation and walkthrough. They require just a little extra reading, experiments or explanation.

**Grp3** Will have acquired the main features of the new substance. The details Flew over in height. They require a good deal more attention to understand the substance well enough.

**Grp4** Will have understood very little of the new substance. It therefore calls for a large, extra effort, so that they can be picked up. Resources which are normally not present. **But in the Knowledge Society, they are there.**

All that is required is teambuilding. Throughout the knowledge-based societies education universe. From Kindergartens to universities.

It is therefore a task for everybody, occupied in teaching , to form education groups into teams.

I don't talk about killing rabbits and frying them on a camp file. Or to run naked around in mud performing weird games. I am talking about teams, where the members work for each others, and with each others. Teams that make sure, that everybody crosses the finishing line. Teams, where one takes responsibility for oneself, and for each others.

Teams needs coaching. This is taken care of by the teachers. The great difference making force in our Knowledge Society is, that members of teams can coach each others. Hence they become *co-coaches.*

There will be members from group. 1 who both can and will help/coach members from group. 2, 3 and 4.

Members from group 2 will rather quickly reach a level, which enables them to help and coach both members from their own group, but also member in group 3 and 4.

Members of group 3 will rarely be able to take part in the co-coaching.

Members of group 4 will probably never take part in co-coaching.

The only demand of students performing co-coaching is: They must do it voluntarily and only on their own, *existing, proved* knowledge.

It is my well consolidated experience, that those, who participate in co-coaching, are enriched by their efforts. At the same time it makes the education groups more homogeneous both socially and in knowledge.

All members of the group will reach a higher learning at optimum time. The teacher is released more quickly to an extra effort for group3 and 4. This is proven knowledge.

When I've talked about group 1, 2, 3 and 4, it must be noted, that these are not static sizes within the class. This is very much dependent on the issue taught. A member from group 4 in one relation could easily belong to group 1 or 2 in other relations. In this way nobody will ever be the *clown of the class*.

Co-coaching uses so far neglected resources and at the same time is freeing other hard-pressed, scarce resources.

I will ask of you to think thoroughly of this unique possibility in your own field. There is so much to be gained by it. And not only within teaching.

### *With the financial cost of absolutely nothing.*

The Mesterlære *), which I heavily recommend reinstated (in Denmark), has always used coaching and co-coaching. It is one of the Mesterlære's strongest forces.

*) Mesterlære.
It is the concept, where you on top of it all has a Master. He is often the owner of the business too.  He has a number of adult, skilled, educated people working for him. Then he has a number of pupils under education. They come on many levels and skills of their own education.
I deeply regret not knowing words for and terminology of the English equivalent on this.

# Coach stock exchange

Let me tell you right away: This is a totally new technique that I developed for furthering the Knowledge Society. Certain informal anomaly of the concept has always existed.

On the stock market the trade is the papers – investments. They are bought and sold mostly in units of single types. Typically, it will be shares from single companies or enterprises. There are also trades of raw materials, cereals, metals and much more.

Where, on the stock market investment objects are the trade, it is knowledge on the *coach stock markets*. Free of charge. Free of risks.

The coach stock market is established in the following way: There is a suitable, nice room to be found. It must feel good to go there. All pupils are invited and are urged to go there. Stock must be open from a half to a whole hour each day. But it is in the end the individual education site, that determines the opening hours. Remember to consult the students on this matter.

On the general stock exchange sales objects will be advertised with a rate. On coach stock exchange will be advertised the individual pupils needs for knowledge. This is a display of need for knowledge on single topics.

All those who come on the stock exchange, will change between the role as coaches and pupils. A pupil, who has knowledge, where another pupil has a need, contacts the latter. Then starts the dissemination of knowledge. The coaching process is underway.

When the lack of knowledge is achieved, the need is deleted from the notice board. A pupil can have an issue hanging over several stock market days.

At some time, the pupil with a need will meet the coach, which will make the lack of knowledge fall into place. Bear in mind the perception strengths and weaknesses.

Coaching on the stock market is an incidence of my own concept co-coaching.

Where co-coaching normally takes place in closed circles around the individual teams, co-coaching on the stock market is much broader.
Here can be obtained knowledge from members of other teams. This will strengthen the formation of the great team, which consists of the entire individual education-site.

It will therefore be a role model for the future society. A society where it is quite natural to have concern for each others. To take responsibility for each others. This change in attitude is very much needed in our modern society.

The coach stock can be implemented on practically all educational institutions. It will release scarce resources. This will optimize the required lead time for the individual education. A substantial saving which is self-financing.

The whole concept is based on student to student relations. Across class, gender and age. We can, however with advantage involve the regular teachers. These can support management and distribution of the coaching. The regular teachers may also in individual cases participate actively in the coaching activities.

There will always be individual pupils, which is ashamed of, or to shy to ask an extra time in the small teams. This is eliminated through the use of a coach stock exchange. Everybody goes there.

# Master class (Mesterlære)

To avoid all the red lights from my computers vocabulary, I transformed the Danish word Mesterlære to the English term Master class. I'm well aware of the fact, that Master class in the rest of the world is something slightly different: One master and a number of students.

This education concept has for a long time been talked very bad about. So bad, that it was thrown on the garbage pile. There is no need to go further into this. Let's look forward.

We should never have rejected Master class. It should have been allowed the undergoing of a process of change. We should instead have made parts of it very different.

*If you want a change, you have to do something different.*

When we think Knowledge Society the Master class fits in excellent.

We will go to the next page in order to hold together related items.

.

A small sketch will be in its place:

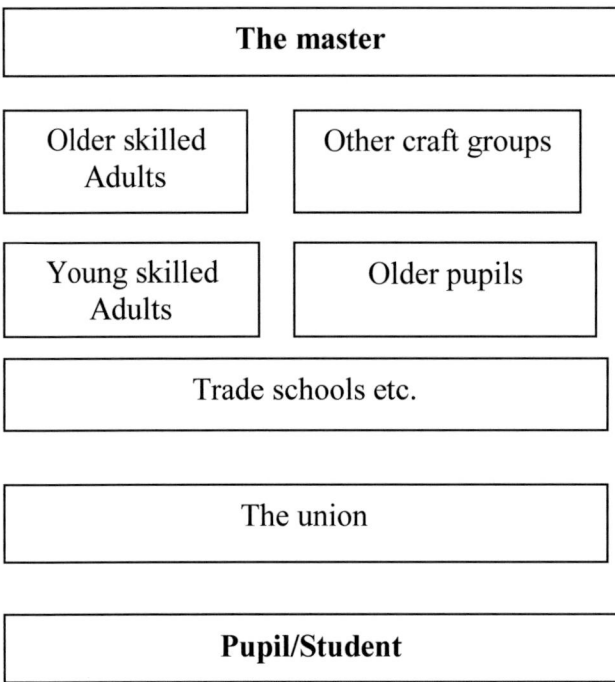

Do you see how nice and applicable this form of the Master class is in a Knowledge Society?
The pupil has a very fine network of coaches and co-coaches at hand, which he can draw upon on practically any issue.

The model, of course, is not necessarily complete for all kind of educations. But it is a clear example to follow.

Outlined is an already existing hierarchy. It is therefore only to make use of it. In the right way.

Business has often complained that there were too high cost of training in apprentices. **It is untrue**. The training must though be tackled in the right way.

In the most educations, perhaps all of them, will pupils could be included in the production apparatus after a relatively short education and training as a beneficial, low cost element.
Pupils must of course train added knowledge. It is best achieved by meaningful training exercises in the form of work, he has already acquired correct knowledge on. This will benefit the pupil, his training and the company.

It is important not to *"over exercise"* the pupil. No overexploitation. He shall not, for example, produce 1200 copies of a certain thing. If there is a need for 1200 copies, let the pupil manufacture the number of copies, which gives him the skill. No more. At least not as a starting point. But of course – if the production of those 1200 copies involves say one o two hours work, using a machine, no harm is done.

Let the pupil work together with older and younger skilled adults. Let the pupil try cooperation with others more skilled pupils. This will give the more experienced pupil training in leadership, work management and coaching.

I urge you to let the pupil return for renewed cooperation with employees, he has worked together with earlier. This gives security for both parts. Remember, that you are right now taking care of an education for a member of a Knowledge Society.

The trade schools should be the supply of proper technical, theoretical knowledge about the profession.

The trade schools should also explain the causal relationships. *So are we doing this because ... This you do, if you will ... etc.*

The trade schools should show the relevant sides of the profession, the trade, which pupils may not be in contact with in the current apprenticeship.

The trade schools must focus very strongly on the trade relevant substance. For example, a smith must be able to understand a technical drawing. He must not be able to produce technical drawings. This is a task of other, competent professionals with up to date, technical tools and skills.

Earlier the pupils were engaged in one particular company during all of the apprenticeship time. The best vocational training institutions had different departments, where pupils could learn more, complementary areas of his forthcoming trade.

This can still be applicable.

Where this is not so, a training can very easy be composed of several different vocational training institutions. Pupils must not, however have a feeling of being torn. He is to be handled kindly, generous and caring in and out of the individual companies.

The apprenticeship for pupils in the individual disciplines and trades must be as short as it is justifiable. Pupils must not pay for their apprenticeship by working as pupils, when they have actually finished their education, training and the Evaluation 3.

**Neither must the time for taking the Evaluation 3 be postponed for any reason at all.**

# Academics

Some people may say that we must assemble some expert groups of academics for analysis and planning. Even for the enforcing activities.

Other people will say quite clearly, that this we must at least not do.

The term academics must not be taken literally. In this context, it covers all highly educated people from all kind of professions.

From this perspective we must definitely use the large group of academics. But they are not to be left alone with the responsibility and all of the work to be done. That would be a fatal disaster in our Knowledge Society. We must remember, a part of the knowledge, possessed by the academics, is based upon commonly, accepted assumptions (old knowledge). But, for that matter, so it is for all people.

Academics have, on an equal footing with other people with knowledge, a legitimate place around the table. It is what it is all about. Nobody has the right, because they have a position, a heading or training. All groups and individuals with  knowledge, which can be used in the creation of a Knowledge Society, has the right to participation in the creation process.

As late as yesterday, I heard a highly estimated earlier top politician use terms such as: *"Everybody know, Everybody want, We all agree on"*. Shame upon him. It is simply very transparent untruths. It is verbal hostage-taking. *It is prohibited.*

We will have to sit down together without any reservation and prejudices. All forms of dividing borderlines in this context anathema (or at least shown off). The same applies The Law of Jante.(explained earlier).

It is not socialism, although it on the positive points may have resemblances with  it. It is public Community. It is society community. This is the strongest force, from where we can collect the necessary energy. Call it like Knowledge-ism for my fault. But there really isn't any need for an ism.

We will not have the knowledge for its own sake. We want knowledge, to create values for the individual and for our society. For Denmark as well as for all the rest of the World.

Well – perhaps the flag got a little well up in the air.

Yes – but that is necessary too.

Without high, achievable ideals called objectives or goals, we will not get very far. And one must of course bear the flag, so that it can be seen by all. I hold it gladly and with pride.

I know, that there are many others too, who would like to be flag bearers. Academics, politicians, trade unions and many, many more. There is a flag for every one of us, who can, and will bear it.

# Elitist Knowledge Society

There could easily be a tendency to think or believe, that a Knowledge Society is for the elite. That we will have the elite in our country to represent or constitute the Knowledge Society. That the Knowledge Society not is for all of us ordinary people.

*It is completely wrong. It is a dangerous point of view!*

It is on the contrary of the utmost importance that the Knowledge Society consists of us all. Yes I am tempted to say that only thus it has its justification. You and I are a part of the Knowledge Society.

However, we can easily use the term elite. It is intended to cover the concept: *The best of the best*. That is where, we have to go. It is our overall objective. That is what we want.

I do not know how many people in this country, which is able to build up a brick wall. To put brick on brick to a perfect wall. A perfect building. I can at least not do it, with the knowledge and skills I possess. That is why we have the bricklayer.

He has obtained knowledge on how to do that kind of work. He has also trained his knowledge. Both through education and practical professional work. He has become an Elitist within his profession. He also has several other competences.

When he is on his scaffolding ready to lay bricks, there are other people, who has prepared his work. Think for example, that the scaffolding he is standing on, is raised properly and safely, by clever, elitist scaffolding workers. These also use all their knowledge, skills and experience. They too are a part of our elite.

The brick layer must also use bricks and mortar. These materials must be present in the right quantities, the right places and on the right time. This task often is done by a bricklayer workman. He is met early on work, to mix mortar of high quality. He has gained knowledge and training in mixing the quite right mortar. The right materials in the right quantities. And through these qualifications, he too belongs to the elite.

Let us just stay a little in construction. If we as a starting point, have a piece of land, where we will have built a house, a plant or anything else, then we must use the Knowledge Society. We are to include many different types of competences from many different disciplines, for that task.

The public sector is also in games with authorisations and controls. Financing require other teams of experts on the track.etc

The short of the long is that the whole project must be borne by knowledge and skills at every stage. People who are elite of their own specialty. The total task is resolved by an elite team. They are working together as a team. They support each other. They have care for each other. That is Knowledge Society.

How clever the individual might be, he knows, that he cannot stand alone. That knowledge he also possesses.

It will therefore not be totally wrong to call the Knowledge Society for Elitist. The elite is just not a small, exclusive enclave. The elite consists of us all.

# Knowledge Society as a religion

The genuine Knowledge Society does not have the slightest resemblance with religion. Nobody must be on their stomach and worship Knowledge Society. The Knowledge Society is the will and not faith. It is recognition of the knowledge's great importance for a good, well-functioning society. For happy, well-functioning people.

The Knowledge Society is not a science. There are though, several persons, who will make it a science. They are wrong. You do not need to carry out research in the concept of Knowledge Society. You have on the other hand all incentives to do research on how we promote the Knowledge Society. You should also conduct research on how we maintain and further develop the Knowledge Society. But that doesn't make it a science in itself. In essence, it is mostly, if not entirely, a matter of common sense.

The Knowledge Society is not a thesis-religion. It is not an ism. The Knowledge Society supports nor the values of ism's. Ism's is based on theses, doctrines, convincing and beliefs. They are based in other words deep in the core on faith. I have said it earlier: Faith is not a part of the Knowledge Society.

Faith is, of course in no way outlawed in the Knowledge Society. A faith can happily live in interaction with the Knowledge Society. Your religion is your own. It must be no taken away from you. It is your clear right to have a faith and a religion.

A second, non religious, use of faith is directly conducive for the Knowledge Society. You can have a belief, that something exists. A context, a reason, an effect and much else. It makes your faith a theory. Theories, we need. They are also an expression of innovation. New thinking.

When you in the research, studies and experiments acquire knowledge, you will get evidence of whether your theory is correct or not. In both cases, have you  acquired useful knowledge which is to the benefit of the Knowledge Society. Have as many theories as you possibly can. But remember to see them to the door with evidence based, factual knowledge.

And share your knowledge.

It is exactly the sharing of knowledge, for which the KBS model is invented. For the sharing and competence acquiring.

# The Knowledge Society model

Is there is a model of the Knowledge Society? No –not really. Basically there is no need to have one. But, it could nevertheless be practical, to have a model in mind when we develop and maintain Knowledge Society.

Here then, is my model:

The model is very simple. It would be very wrong though, to complicate the overall model more than the here above shown.

When we have taken the decision, that we want the Knowledge Society, there will be a need for many sub models. The more detailed these models will be, the more toward the real planning and working basis for implementation we will get.

Would it be helpful if I gave some supplementary comments on the model? All right then:

## The Knowledge Society Model (we could shorten it to the KSM)..

- **Acquire existing knowledge** – All around us there is already existing, collected knowledge. We must acquire that knowledge, when needed and applicable. The obvious reason for that is that knowledge is the real value in the KS. And we shouldn't all reinvent the deep plate and the hot water (Danish saying), since it is already done.
- **Find new knowledge** – In spite of the huge amount of knowledge already found, we have a lot of blank spots in that knowledge. These GAP's we must seek closed. When you turn one stone, a new "world" is revealed. There too we must probe. The same goes for all the brilliant ideas and theories that pops up in our innovative heads. And into all of that, of which existence we have absolutely no idea of, as of today.Yet.
- **Pass knowledge** – In the KS the knowledge is in no way precious marvels, which we must keep to ourselves. Both you and the KS gets richer when you share your knowledge with others. When you give it away to whom it will become new competences. Knowledge is not a drug. It must therefore be free for everybody to acquire and use. Of course, the passing of knowledge doesn't have to be free of charge. But this is a total different story.

- **Use knowledge** – Could I have lost all my marvels? Have I a carousel, where my brain should be? No – so far from that. On the contrary. Look around you and be amazed over the many instances where you see people act, without actually using their own, existing knowledge. You even will discover cases of acting *against* possessed knowledge. But the far more wrong issue is: ***It is not only done by individuals.*** Our highly esteemed business does it. It is done in the public offices. Your local city council does it. It is done in government offices. To shorten or end the list: *It is done everywhere at all levels in our society.* And you know it. This must we - will we - do something about.

When you have swallowed the above pills, and you start feeling the reaction on them, can you see that my model KSM has the right size? The exact needed number of modules? That nothing needs to be added?

After reading my book you are capable of sitting in any forum with your work gloves on, and actually create the Knowledge Society.

Be you in any position in our society:

# You know what you must do, and you know how to do it!

# When do we get the Knowledge Society?

*We don't get it! We will never get it! We are creating it! Period.*

A Knowledge Society is a very large, live, man created organism. Not abstract but visible and tangible. It consists of people with competences. Of many people with many competences.

The Knowledge Society requires research. But research also requires a Knowledge Society. They are inextricably linked. Without research no Knowledge Society and vice versa. But it starts at a completely different place.

The creation of a Knowledge Society will start with the child. Our only, necessary raw material. Here we must make our first major effort.
.
The child's first education is given by its parents. The importance of this education cannot be emphasized enough. This importance, must both be pointed out and be given priority. It is the basis and foundation for all subsequent education. What does this imply?

This means that parents must *coach* their children. They must give them security, care, love and knowledge. They must make them ready to join and participate in our society as team members.

There are so much which you as parents can teach your child. As we, as parents, have the competence to teach about. I am not competent to make a complete list of what parents can and must teach their children. I can only come up with some examples. So that I'll do.

Here at least, *you* can be an excellent coach and teacher to your child:

- Personal hygiene.
- Cleanliness of what is being circumvented.
- Cleaning up after ended up activities.
- Everything has its place.
- Everything has its time.
- Obedience.
- Care for themselves.
- Concern and care for others.
- To ask for help
- To provide help
- Ensure compliance with agreements
- Ensure compliance with times.
- Playing alone and with others
- To ask.
- To be honest.
- Difference on yours and mine.
- Good treatment of, and in the wild.
- Good treatment of animals.
- Satisfy own needs after ability.
- To find borders.
- Respecting borders.
- And very, very much more.

Parents and other experts must make this list complete themselves. It is as such my primary bid for what you as parent, most certainly can teach your child.

The child is the person who is handed in for care and education in kindergartens, nursery school, 0-te class and public schools etc. These places the children should enter sliding smoothly. These institutions must not have the obligation to, nor the need for, to carry out the parents education obligations.

**Maturation of the child to the meeting with society is the responsibility solely of the parents.**

If the child is properly matured by its parents, will it from the outset be both giving an receptive in the Knowledge Society. So you see: It is starting early with the child.

What about all of us, who are not children?

We are those who have to create the Knowledge Society. We must take many decisions, which leads to the Knowledge Society. We must become skilled persons. We need to achieve more personal competences.

But we need just as much to become skilled in order to be able to give others more competences. These competences must be based on real knowledge. We must therefore become skilled individuals. We must also obtain knowledge in order to achieve the great sense of joy by acquired, applicable knowledge.

We must help to the creation of positive motivations for the acquisition of knowledge in all of our society.

We must identify and to use positive carrots throughout the process of transformation toward the Knowledge Society.

We must recognize the wholly ineffective Whipping everywhere we see it. Then we need to abandon the whip and replace it with the far more efficient carrots.

We must ensure that knowledge will be achieved by want instead of coercion, fear, duty and horror

The delight in applicable knowledge is so strong that it must not be underestimated as motivation in itself.

There is also much work related to preparation for a Knowledge Society.

Just the work to create knowledge based job requirement specifications is great. It is, of course those, which provides the basis for composition of knowledge based evaluations and educations. A positive side effect of job requirement specifications is, that it creates knowledge and overview of the jobs, work or education covered.

The job requirement analyzes can usually be split up into smaller quantities. These are to be linked together later, to form a coherent job requirement specification.

Thus can we already by now, make a great difference. And we must do so.

The reference to the children's role is also due to them being our future trend setters.

There is therefore a wide-ranging public upbringing to take place. This needs our society very much. People who move around in our society, in a good and safe way, out of desire for doing so, because they feel that it is the right.
Not because some law requires it.

We must setup both short- and long-term objectives. We must achieve the set objectives. We must feel both personal and national pride and success. It is the best *drive* for a better future.

So – when do we have a Knowledge Society?

We .have it instantly at the very moment we starts up the process of transformation. Not the huge, all encompassing, Knowledge Society, that we want to be a reality. The creation of a Knowledge Society must be based on knowledge. That is why it comes to live right from the outset. We have born the Knowledge Society, when we have taken the decision that it is what we will have.

I have given some practical instructions and recommendations on how I see the creation process. If others know better than me, then we must listen to them. And we must use them.

My very loud plea is this:

***Put on the work clothes! Take decisions! Make the planning! Supply resources! Follow the plans to the objectives are reached!***

# The end

It has been a pleasant and giving activity to write this book. It has given me the opportunity to use large parts of my own knowledge. I have also been given an opportunity to put my knowledge into a structured context. Otherwise this book wouldn't have made any sense.

I have been forced to make acid test of my knowledge. When all the filling was etched away, was I then left with real and genuine knowledge? Only knowledge, which graduated this test, is included in the book. So it should therefore also have a great value for you.

It has been one of my objectives to create a result rewarding society debate on Knowledge Society. Such a debate is best initiated, if you have something concrete, as this book, to deal with as a starting point.

If I have disseminated knowledge, which can be rejected with evidence to the contrary, you are most welcome to tell me.

I expect some punches on my nose, to have put my snout so deeply into our society. So take your punch at me. I can take it.

Before you strike me, I will ask of you to reflect thoughtful deep inside yourself.

Things can appear difficult or impossible, just because we never have tried them before. But we must do much new and different
.

## *If you do, as you use to do, the result will be the usually!*

# Appendix

Now I'm going to talk about an education of a billiard player. To be more specific, a DK5PB player. The education is constructed as my best bet on an education which is aiming at the Knowledge Society.

In the construction of this education I've made use of most of my gathered knowledge and experiences within education in general.

I have gathered experiences from many, very different kind of trades. This include my own education and my jobs in the army of managing and as an instructor.

*High Performance* which I'll be referencing, is a very extensive course, where I have participated.
The purpose of the course was, in my later rationalized assessment, to find out what is required, in order to provide *high performance.* Throughout the course ran a current of an increased awareness and a fact based injection of the necessary knowledge. The course was in this way the achievement of a functioning, self generating Knowledge Society.

The course was given by the DDBU (The Danish Billiard Union) with Dan Nielsen as the instructor.

Once again I must remind you, that even though billiard may be tedious to you, I've only used it as the carrier - the KBS model - to have a load to work with. For your possibility to link praxis with theory.

# High Performance

Job requirements analyzes for DK5PB.
February 29 2009

In this analyzes there will be focus on four requirement areas:
- Physical requirements
- Psychic requirements
- Tactical requirements
- Technical requirements

## Physical requirements

There are very few physical requirements, if what counts is only to have pleasure by playing billiard.
Since this level of ambition is too low, regarding High performance, I will look at the requirements aimed at this level.

## Physical size and age

In order to play sufficiently relaxed, it is my experience, that a minimum height of 130 – 140 cm. is necessary. Is it less, it will be difficult to get a useful overview of the individual dessins on the billiard table.
There will also be to many dessines, where you cannot obtain the required, relaxed physical positions for, and the execution of the shots. The aiming function will be more difficult due to lack of overview from sufficient height.

The age should be minimum 12 to 14 years. This is, however in no way unequivocally. It is far more a question of having the sufficient maturity.

One must be able to setup objectives, to have visions, to perform serious training and to suffer deprivations.

The sight must be sufficiently good on distances from ½ to 2½ m.

One must be able to bend forward, down, to a position where the chin is almost touching the queue.

One must not suffer from shakings which prevents a calm body attitude, aim and shot.

One must have full freedom of movements in hand, elbow and shoulder.

One must have a sufficient good physical condition to be able to stand up in 3 times 1 and a half hours, without this having negative affects one's ability of body attitudes, aim and shot, or that it weakens one's concentration.

It has, of course been proved in several cases, that people with even significant disabilities have been very skilful billiard players.

## Psychic requirements

The Psychic requirements are of concern in a good deal of different areas in this kind of sport.
The requirements will though be correlating with requirements for other disciplines and other kinds of sport.

I will particularly concentrate my analyzes towards these two areas:
- Training
- Match

## Training

Before you begin a training session, you must make it quite clear to yourself: What will you train, how will you train, for how long time will you train and how will you measure the results of your training.
(This in some cases is up to your instructor or trainer versus coach).

You must focus totally and exclusively on these issues.

Prepare yourself and your equipment calmly with the seriousness, as if you wore preparing yourself for playing a very important match.

Execute your training strictly following the planning. Do not allow yourself to be disturbed and divert from your plan.

Have enough self discipline to execute your entire program.

You have to be careful to note the results of your training in the form of measure points in your Game Plan. This is the only thing that can give you certainty on the impact of your training.

You must teach yourself, that your training is of equally great importance for you, as your tournament matches.

## Match

I would distinguish between training matches and tournament matches. Training matches is not "fun-matches".

Fun-matches are important for the relaxation. You can play with funny combinations and extreme dessins. They can have the same positive effect as the warming up exercise. They can help you remove stiffness from your body and your play. They give you also the opportunity for relaxed social interaction with your comrades across all divisions such as age, skill, gender etc.

## Training match

Training matches are important for your opportunity to enter a match condition without the negative impact of a poor result.

You have to use your preparation for training matches to train your preparation for tournament matches.

It would be best for you, if you for some of your training matches, performed those dressed up in the Regulatory "battle dress". This will help you to interconnect the clothes with match importance. But the most important thing is that it will tear the fatal out of the tournament matches represented by the "battle dress".

Use the many advantages of a training match. You can use "time out", replay, set-matches instead of full distance and many other discrepancies, to promote the value of a training match. But – a great deal of your training matches must be executed as a true copy of a tournament match, in as many aspects as possible.

## Tournament match

Tournament matches is, after all, what it is all about.

Before you begin to play in large, open tournaments and final rounds, the most of your matches will be 1 match per day. Either as an individual or as a team Member.

Tournament matches can place quite specific psychological pressure on your shoulders.

You may have travelled a long distance and for many hours, to play this one match.
It is perhaps only a victory, which will bring you further in the competition.
The match may be the issue of up - or relegation. Or season victory?
Or one of the many other reasons for this match to be very important for you.

**But before it is played, it is actually a match, just like all other matches.**

It therefore requires all of your acquired and trained preparations for a match. But nothing else and nothing more.

See to a good, physical wellbeing through all the parameters, that taught you, what works for you. Rest, diet, beverage, the toilet, good bye to the family, check on the travel schedule, dressing, money, starting admission, show up in good time, bath, jogging and much, much more – or some completely different things. *What works for you?*

All of this will create a state of psychological calmness and stability within you. This will help you in the worst of all: The fear of losing.

Remember – when you are about to play – you will use the most of what you have spent so much time on learning and training, to achieved competences.

You have *all* you need in your accompanied "toolbox".
That goes for everything physically, you will use at the table, as well as what you will use psychologically.
Your tools for tension regulation.
Your ability to remain uninfluenced by your own or your opponents play.

Your opponent may have made many flukes, He may have been lucky in many situations. But after all, it has nothing to do with you. It is not the result of errors, you have made. You haven't had any influence on it. So all you have to do is a recharging in order to do your best, when it is your turn again. *What can't be cured must be endured!*

Should your turn not come or be insufficient, you have just got a little "present" from your opponent. You have gained knowledge of at least one, but probably more details that you can bring back to your training program. And after all, that is not so bad?

It may be good for you, during the match, to make a short note of the nature of the error, you made. You could have been put in an almost impossible situation. If it is given to you by your opponent, ignore it. But if you created the situation, note what went wrong in the previous shot.

There may be many different, disruptive factors during a match. Common to all of them: They really do not have a decisive impact on your game. You are in your own battle zone. There, nothing can interfere with you. It may delay you a little, but – it can do no harm to you. Or your play. Because as we say as of today: You are in *flow*.

If an injustice is made to you, point it out in great calm. But don't do anything further.

I will close the issue here. More examples could be displayed in order to emphasize the major role of the psyche.

## Tactical requirements

The tactical requirement in DK5PB is actually quite few.
The superior tactic in the game has primary 2 demands: You must score in every shot, and you must be able to continue. So it is in most of the billiard games and disciplines.

There are some parameters, that you can adjust in your choice of a dessin:
- Shortest possible rolling of the balls for scoring **AND** giving a good after shot.
- Easiest dessin for a score, **AND** a good after shot.
- Always a cushion in the dessin, provided that this will not spoil the after shot.
- A dessin which can give a double position (a situation where both of the white object balls are between the pins and your red queue ball).

- Never make a carambole (queue ball hitting both object balls) AND pins for the joy of the extra four points. Can of course be accepted if it will close the set or the match.
- Avoid long distance between the queue ball and the first object ball.

In case of a practically impossible layout of the balls, or the percentage chance for a score is very low, choose a dessin that makes it difficult for your opponent too. This isn't unfair but conscious defence. Just look at the safety play in a snooker match.

## Technical requirements

The technical requirements can be divided into some groups or subjects:

- Required tools in the physical toolbox
- Tempo control
- Draw- and follow-control including point of aim calculations
- Understanding of the effect on "English" in the queue ball
- The usage of various bridges (ways of holding and controlling the queue with the forehand)
- The usage of different shot or queue techniques
- Aiming point calculation (no – I don't repeat myself)
- Weakening and strengthening of queue ball resp. 1. object ball on follow- and draw-shots
- Knowledge of the pins effect on the object ball at contact from different angles
- The "Diamond" system for "quarters" in 3 cushion carambole for usage in pre- cushion shots over more than 2 cushions
- Control of the billiard table compared to a table without discrepancies

The above list should be extended to encompass all thinkable, technical requirements excluding "art" billiard and show-of-shots. This is to increase the understanding of the many elements, which has influence on the outcome of a shot and the choice of a dessin.

The more complete this list is, the fewer events could be called luck or accidents.

## Required tools in the physical toolbox

I am talking about the many possible types of dessins.: (In the Appendix 2 I'll give you my description of the DK5PB including the names of the dessin types). OB equals the first white object ball.

- *Direct* — OB goes directly into the pin area without touching a cushion first.
- *Peak* — OB goes through short and long cushion into the pin area.
- *Double Peak* — OB goes through short, long, short and long cushion into the pin area (around the table).
- *Across* — OB goes through long cushion into the pin area.
- *Double Across* — OB goes through long and long cushion into the pin area.
- *Long* — OB goes through short cushion into the pin area.
- *Double Long* — OB goes through short and short cushion into the pin area.
- *Quarter* — OB goes through long, short and long cushion into the pin area.
- *High Peak* — OB goes through long and short cushion into the pin area.
- *Pin play.* — The king of it all. The object balls are circulated round the pin area in tight played dessins.

Maybe the list should include more types of dessins but those are the most commonly used.

The list contains possibilities for both scoring on the individual dessin, but also to improve the positions towards a *direct* or the *double position* in the after shot.

It is important, that all of the above mentioned dessins are learned to their full extent.

How little is the smallest *quarter* that can be played?
Where are the aiming lines between the smallest and the largest?
Can the variance be extended by the use of "English"?
By follow- or draw-shot?
Or by a combination of both "English" and draw- or follow-shot?
What is the effect of tempo?
What if the object ball is placed pressed against or very close to the first cushion?

I do not wish to extend the requirement analysis for now. Not because it isn't necessary. It shouldthough not be a one-mans-work. You will get the greatest value, if it consists of more peoples accumulated knowledge.

I have not sought to fill the content by assistance of textbooks or other source material.
This is because if I only lists, what others have already expressed their views upon, then there is no renewal or new approaches.

## A little summing up

This was my example of a requirement analysis for the job or trade as a Pin Billiard Player.

The total game is exploded into atoms to acquire knowledge. Then all the atoms are linked together one by one to manageable quantities. These in turn becomes the Job Requirement Specifications. Those descriptions are used to form Evaluation 1, educational lessons, training programs and training plans (Game Plans).

I think that it is about time to show an example of an education in a single discipline (dessin) with the accompanied Game Plan.

By the way: Did anyone claim, that billiard is a simple sport?

# Education on one subject

The following I have brought in as a copy from one of my text books in the series *I will learn!* These text books are in the booklet form. They each deal with one and only one subject. They have quite a few common characteristics, so that the readers and pupils soon will feel eased and at home in this form of education.

To seek an education form, a systematic or a structure which can be repeated wholly or very closely, in a long term education, is very important. It will bring the pupil security and a distinct feeling of security.
Learning in an atmosphere of security is without discussion the most conducive. No unnecessary resources are used to obtain for instance an overview of the incalculable.

Remember, that the previously mentioned upfront orientation on the near and the distant objectives for the education, is part of creating the sense of security.

On reading and use of my text books on billiard education, you will once again see the term Game Plan. By now you already know what is meant by that term. I have used this term in order to stay in the terminology amongst those seriously interested in knowledge based education within the billiard universe.

So: Education on one subject!

# I will learn to play peaks over 2 cushions!

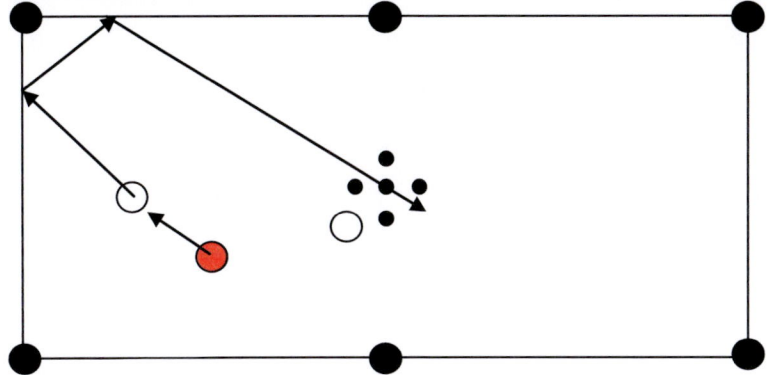

Instruktor: Kjeld Reby Løren

# First time peaks in general

Now our subject is peaks or first time peaks or peaks over 2 cushions'. A bellowed child has many names, but they all apply to the same: An object ball played via a short cushion and a long cushion to the pin area.

For calculation of the object balls running lane and aiming points, we will use the diamonds and my table for peaks. There are six standard peaks, which all must be played with tempo. Tempo means in this case, that the object ball reaches the pin area, runs through it, and not much further. It may under no circumstances pass the *salvo line* behind the pins.

You shall, in this lesson, play the queue bal in R6,1 or R6,2. This will be an amorti (killing) draw shot or a limited draw shot.

You place both balls on the specified lines in the table such as the line 20-22; Put the red and white ball, so that they are comfortable to play.

Exercise these six dessins and make yourself confident with the tempo play. Tempo must always be part of a dessin, and you must always plan your tempo.

Use the attached Game Plan to record your training and your progress.

When you are familiar with playing these 6 standard tempo peaks, we will see what happens when we play very hard.

# The six standard peaks

The following 6 diamonds on the long cushion is connected with 6 equivalent diamond points on the short cushion:

| Long cushion | Short cushion |
|:---:|:---:|
| 10 | 14 |
| 20 | 22 |
| 30 | 30 |
| 40 | 34 |
| 50 | 37 |
| 60 | 40 |

If the character of the shot and the tempo is correct, but the object ball passes the pin area without scoring, it is due to differences in the table (the cushions or the cloth) from a standard table. This must then be adjusted accordingly in the aiming point at the short cushion.

It may though also be due to the fact, that you unintended has played the dessin diverting from the pointed out aiming line, or have played the queue ball with "English".

Any dessin, that you want to test, can be played with the queue ball alone. The shot then has to be in the point R12,2. This gives the queue ball an effect, corresponding to the played, white ball.

On the drawing is shown the smallest and the largest peak, that can be played with normal, neutral shot technique.
See how this is shown in the table above.

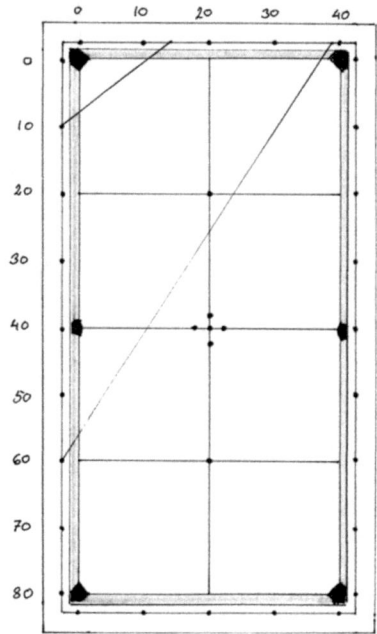

The six aiming lines, which I have calculated, all starts from whole diamond numbers on the long cushion. 10, 20, 30 etc. Those you will easily remember. The diamond numbers on the short cushion is a little more difficult to remember. Try to see, if you can find an easy way to remember or memorize them. You are allowed to have them on a small note in your pocket.

## Game Plan 1 the standard peak

Here is your Game Plan for training peaks (via 2 cushions).
The columns 1 to 10 correspond to 10 individual days of training.
For each day and each dessin you must note, how many times out of five,
you played it perfectly.
All dessins must be played 5 times.
Thus you can make a score of 0 to 5 points per dessin.
This equals 30 shots in your training.

| Position of balls | 1 | 2 | 3 | 4 | 5 | 6 | 7 | 8 | 9 | 10 |
|---|---|---|---|---|---|---|---|---|---|---|
| Line 10 - 14 | | | | | | | | | | |
| Line 20 - 22 | | | | | | | | | | |
| Line 30 - 30 | | | | | | | | | | |
| Line 40 - 34 | | | | | | | | | | |
| Line 50 - 37 | | | | | | | | | | |
| Line 60 - 40 | | | | | | | | | | |

Below you note which date you executed this part of your Game Plan.

| Day | Date | Day | Date |
|---|---|---|---|
| 1 | | 6 | |
| 2 | | 7 | |
| 3 | | 8 | |
| 4 | | 9 | |
| 5 | | 10 | |

Have a pleasant training.

# The peak played hard

Now you have seen and learned how to play the peak with tempo. Do you see that my table is well suited as a starting point?

So what will happen, if you play the peak hard?
The first difference you will observe is that the short cushion kicks the object ball hard down along the table. This does, that all of my dessins from the table will be too large for a standard peak.

Here is what you must do, if you want to play the peak hard:

A hard played peak cannot be played further down the long cushion than diamond number 40.

You diamond points and aiming lines will therefore bee:

| 10 | 19 | *) |
|----|----|----|
| 20 | 27 | |
| 30 | 35 | |
| 40 | 40 | |

*) Will often score from behind (via 4 cushions) if it passes the pin area the first time.

What is the purpose of playing a peak hard?
There could be several reasons for doing so.
You might want to play the first object ball down and close to the second object ball. This in order to continue with a carambole.
Another could be, that you want to play the object ball back on the same half of the table, where it came from.

Some of the peaks played hard, will end up being another peak, a good *quarter*, an easy *across* or maybe even a *direct*.

The hard played peak will run very differently up the table from the second short cushion. Try to see these lines on the 4 dessins in my table. You might want to make a note on these resulting lines.

To play a peak hard is almost always a plan of emergency. This is because the concept of *hard* is very floating. How hard is hard? It is in the line of 'a bit' and 'quite' etc.

You will never achieve the good and floating game, if you do not learn how to master the tempo play.

But as I said: Playing hard is not exclusively negative.

## Game Plan 2 peak played hard

Here is your Game Plan for training hard played peaks.

The columns 1 to 10 correspond to 10 individual days of training.
For each day and each dessin you must note, how many times out of five,
you played it perfectly.
All dessins must be played 5 times.
Thus you can make a score of 0 to 5 points per dessin.
This equals 20 shots in your training.

| Position of balls | 1 | 2 | 3 | 4 | 5 |
|---|---|---|---|---|---|
| Line 10 – 19 | | | | | |
| Line 20 – 27 | | | | | |
| Line 30 – 35 | | | | | |
| Line 40 – 40 | | | | | |

Below you note which date you executed this part of your Game Plan.

| Day | Date |
|---|---|
| 1 | |
| 2 | |
| 3 | |
| 4 | |
| 5 | |

Have a pleasant training.

# The peak played as a cut ball

On my course's and in my text books I have drawn the attention to the subject *ball-effect*.

When the queue ball hits the object ball to the right or to the left of the centre point, the object ball will obtain a *ball-effect*. As if the object ball was played with "English". This may have a negative of positive effect on your dessin. The effect is seen clearest, when the object ball hits the first cushion.

I have now investigated, which effect this has on the 6 standard peaks played as cut balls:

## *It has in practise no bothering effect.*

If you cut the object ball in a tempo play, the result is so little deviating, that you can disregard it.

Quite different though, if you play *both* hard and cuts. This will involve so many factors, that the outcome is impossible to give precise specifications on.

I'll advice you to train some cut peaks with tempo. After all, you have to predict the running lanes of the queue ball after contact with the OB.

Your Game Plan for this will be equal to your first Game Plan.
This you need not train for more than five days. Then you will know, that it works, as I have explained.

## Game Plan 3 the peak as a cut ball

Here is your Game Plan for training cut' peaks (via 2 cushions).
The columns 1 to 10 correspond to 10 individual days of training.
For each day and each dessin you must note, how many times out of five,
you played it perfectly.
All dessins must be played 5 times.
Thus you can make a score of 0 to 5 points per dessin.
This equals 30 shots in your training.

The new issue is, that **the lines in the table below applies only to the
object ball**. You must place the queue ball to the left or right of the lines.
You decide the angle of the cutting. Try both left and right to the lines. Do
some experiments here.

| Position of obj. Ball | 1 | 2 | 3 | 4 | 5 |
|---|---|---|---|---|---|
| Line 10 - 14 | | | | | |
| Line 20 - 22 | | | | | |
| Line 30 - 30 | | | | | |
| Line 40 - 34 | | | | | |
| Line 50 - 37 | | | | | |
| Line 60 - 40 | | | | | |

| Day | Date |
|---|---|
| 1 | |
| 2 | |
| 3 | |
| 4 | |
| 5 | |

How to fill in the above two tables, you already know.

Have a pleasant training.

## The peak played as an *under-hand* ball

An *under-hand* ball is not new to you. Just my naming convention.

An under-hand ball is also a cut ball. It is harder to explain this, than it is to show it to you. Look at the sketch below:

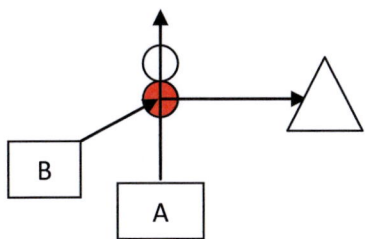

When you shoot the queue ball from position A directly towards the object ball we call this a *straight on.* When you shoote the queue ball from position B we call it an *under-hand.* In both cases will the resulting direction of the object ball be the same. This, of course, is not the same for the queue ball.

## *This has in practice no harmful effect.*

With one exception: The first dessin 10-14 has to be played as 10-15.

If you cut the object ball in a tempo play, the result for the other five dessins is so little deviating, that you can disregard it.

Quite different again though, if you play *both* hard and under-hand. This will involve so many factors, that the outcome is impossible to give precise specifications on.

I'll advice you to train these under-hand cut peaks with tempo. After all, you have to predict the running of the queue ball.

On the first 3 dessins it will often be quite easy to draw the queue ball down behind the pin area to a new, good position on the other half of the table.

On the other 3 dessins it will often be easier to keep the queue ball at the same half part of the table, from where the dessin is played.

But the solution depends entirely on the position of all three balls before the shot.

## Game Plan 4 peak as an *under-hand* ball

Here is your Game Plan for training peaks (via 2 cushions) as under-hands.
The columns 1 to 10 correspond to 10 individual days of training.
For each day and each dessin you must note, how many times out of five,
you played it perfectly.
All dessins must be played 5 times.
Thus you can make a score of 0 to 5 points per dessin.
This equals 30 shots in your training.

**You** will on these exercises determine the position of the queue ball on each
dessin.

| Position of cue ball | 1 | 2 | 3 | 4 | 5 |
|---|---|---|---|---|---|
| Line 10 - **15** | | | | | |
| Line 20 - 22 | | | | | |
| Line 30 - 30 | | | | | |
| Line 40 - 34 | | | | | |
| Line 50 - 37 | | | | | |
| Line 60 - 40 | | | | | |

| Day | Date |
|---|---|
| 1 | |
| 2 | |
| 3 | |
| 4 | |
| 5 | |

Fill in the tables above in the same way you did with the former tables.

Enjoy your training.

# End of education on one subject

This was in broad terms, what I can teach you about playing *peaks*.
I am not at this time in possession of  much more knowledge about precisely
this type of dessin. And yet. I know at least one more thing.

It is about the use of "English". This will change the outgoing angle from
the first hit cushion. This means that you can waste a peak played according
to my table specifications completely. It will either be too large or too small.

But that is not the whole truth.

Because you can also use "English" for something positive.

If you have a ball line, that almost fits your purpose, but just not quite, you
can use "English" for an adjustment. By this tool you can either open or
close the outgoing angle from the cushion.

It works like this: Play the queue ball in the left side, and the queue ball will
rotate clockwise. After contact between the two balls, the object ball will
rotate counter clockwise. And vice versa.

In this way you can open or close the angle of the object ball on contact
with the cushion. Do you see the point? Of course you do.

# End of education on one subject (2)

I do not expect that you, as a reader, has the great interest in the Danish Five Pin Billiard, or billiard in general, if any at all.

Billiard is though one of my major sport interests.

But this should be crystal clear to you by now: If you will learn to play based on knowledge instead of hunches and natural talent, Then there is a lot in fact, that **can** be learned. That is the essence of my examples.

Could you see the continuous, effective systematic?

This is a known, systematic road to reach the objectives. A road that works. The only requirement is, that you have to choose that road. And you have to follow that road in loyalty to your objectives. Half-hearted does not work.

I will now continue with an example of an Evaluation 1, fetched from my billiard world.

# Evaluation 1 prior to a billiard education

Following is the Evaluation 1 of the pupil to be. This evaluation must be taken prior to the beginning of the education.

The evaluation must be summary, covering the total area, where the pupil wants progress. In this case it is the discipline called pin billiard in its total.

The purpose is, as mentioned earlier, to find the strengths and weaknesses in the pupil's knowledge and skills. Based on this knowledge, a real education plan can be put to together covering the concerned subjects, into a total Game Plan.

The total Game Plan is divided into manageable smaller Game Plans. Those will become the pupil's education- and training sessions.

# High Performance Evaluation 1

Pupil:                          John Doe

Date of evaluation:             mm.dd.yyyy

Controlling coach:              Jane Hername

This evaluation will set focus on the following four areas of requirements:

- Physical requirements
- Psychic requirements
- Tactical requirements
- Technical requirements

## Physical requirements

To be answered either with an OK or a short comment.

| Requirement | Status |
|---|---|
| Adequate height | |
| Age / Maturity | |
| Sight | |
| Mobility of the body | |
| Steady hand | |
| Movement of hand, elbow and shoulder | |
| Physical condition *) | |

These are all "soft" values. Accurate measures are not needed.
*) The overall physical condition including possible disabilities.

# Psychic requirements

To be answered with an approximate percentage in relation to the optimum.

| Training: | Status |
|---|---|
| Focus on session curriculum | |
| Result registration | |
| Seriousness as in a match | |
| To follow the planning in total | |
| | |
| **Match** | |
| Differ between fun- and training matches | |
| Able to build up the optimum level of tension | |
| Able to regulate the tension before and during a match | |
| Same seriousness as in training | |
| Concentration | |
| Meet the match as open, with equal possibilities | |
| | |
| **Tournament** | |
| Relax between matches | |
| "Recharge" before each match | |
| | |
| **Leisure and other activities** | |
| Participation in those 100 % | |

These are to be best estimates.

# Tactical requirements

To be answered with an approximate percentage in relation to the optimum.

| Requirements | Status |
|---|---|
| Able to see relevant dessins | |
| Chose best progressive dessin | |
| Shortest, possible ball movement | |
| The easiest dessin, if it is progressive | |
| Preferably a cushion in each dessin | |
| Work towards the "double position" and directs | |
| Never carambole for the 4 extra points (and yet) | |
| Short distance between queue ball and 1. Object ball | |
| Play safe on impossible dessins | |

These too are to be best estimates.

# Technical requirements

To be answered with an approximate percentage in relation to the optimum.

| Requirements | Status |
|---|---|
| Tempo control | |
| Draw- and follow- control incl. Aiming point calculation | |
| Understand the impact of "English" in queue ball | |
| Usage of different "bridges" | |
| Usage of different shot techniques | |
| Aiming point calculations in general | |
| Weakening/fortifying the queue ball/object ball on draw- and follow-shots | |
| Knowledge of impact on object ball on contact with the pin area | |
| Diamond system RC 2000 for usage in pre cushion shots | |
| Control of the table in comparison with a table without deviations | |
| Across dessins via 1 and 2 cushions | |
| Along dessins via 1 and 2 cushions | |
| Peaks via 2 cushions | |
| Peaks via 4 cushions | |
| Traditional quarters | |
| Follow – quarters | |
| High peak | |
| Under-hand balls along and across the table | |

The evaluations of the Technical requirements are containing a mixture of soft and hard values. The soft values is the students view of his own skills versus the requirements. The teacher, or some other competent person, must coach the pupil during the responding, in order to have the most truthful answer, when the need for coaching arises.

The hard values show the existing, technical skills. These are not a question of opinions, but direct, measurable values. Once again the pupil is to be assisted by the teacher, or another, competent person.

For all the technical requirements are quite specific exercises with clearly defined, expected results (not shown in this book).

Remember always, that this is an exploratory evaluation. Pupils must not be expected to master any of the substance. He has not yet been brought correct knowledge, which he has been able to train into skills or competences.

On certain educations, Evaluation 1 can be an excellent way to the fragmentation of optimum groups on the basis of uniform knowledge/skills. This breakdown may only apply the initial education and training.

Later cooperation of the minor teams into one team must take place. The importance of teams in the context of education, I showed in my covering of Coaching and coaches.

# Game Plans

When the real education starts, it must follow a clear, transparent plan. This is absolutely essential. As you already now so well by now, I use the term Game Plan for a well defined setup for both education, training and result registration
If a specific training has a need of the possibility to extempore, to divert in a controlled manner from the straight course, the actual planning must take account of this.

In order to show proof of the efficiency of my KBS mode, I created a scenario, where the measuring of the result was possible.

Here are my setup conditions and my Game Plans:

## Game Plan summer 2009

## Student:    Kjeld Reby Løren

Due to my age, it isn't of relevance to setup a Game Plan covering several years.
It is unpredictable to what degree; my physical capabilities will spoil such ambitions.

I therefore have chosen to make a three month Game Plan. It is my intention to make a new three month Game Plan, before the expiry of the first one.

My Game Plan only deals with my will of change on the technical requirements. That is where I see the greatest lacks in my present competences.
The psychic training though, will be an extension parallel to the physical training. Only is it not timetabled.

My Game Plan involves 3 weekly training sessions. Those will be named: Day 1, day 2 and day 3.

Each daily session will be at the length of 2 hours.

Those will be divided into 4 part sessions with a duration of 30 minutes.

The first part session is a specific, technical discipline like for instance a peak over two cushions.

The second part session is always the break-of as a peak with the continuation of series build-up (breaks in snooker).

The third part session is again a specific, technical discipline like for instance a peak over four cushions.

The fourth part session is series build-up (breaks in snooker) from a fixed, ideal position of both the queue ball and the two object balls in relation to the pin area.

The content of each part session is thoroughly described with (starting) positions, tempo demands and measure points.

The result of the executions of each part element is registered immediately for a subsequent evaluation.

If sufficient degree of perfection is achieved in a discipline, the Game Plan is revised.

This particular Game Plan is to be seen as maintenance and extension of already achieved competences. After all, I'm obviously not a novice in the game.

It is also a means for the improvement of inadequate technical skills.

It is **NOT**, and this is very important, a learning process for someone completely new in the game.

The starting point for this Game Plan is my requirement specifications. Through the Evaluation 1 it showed clearly, where I had my GAP's, my weaknesses.

The technique may, after my best conviction, be used by players at every level except for the absolutely new ones..

# Day 1 part session 1

## Curriculum              Peak via 2 cushions

It is to be played from diamond 10 – 60 on the long cushion.
The object ball must pass the pin area and end in the 8. part of the table
following the pin area.
Start with queue and object ball in a comfortable distance from the long
cushion.

After a correct, executed shot on all 6 diamonds, you should vary the
distance between the balls and the distance to the cushion (if and when time
allows).

Register the number of approved attempts per. diamond.
Execute 5 attempts per. diamond

D = Diamond, 1=10, 2=20 etc.

| Date.. | D1 | D1 | D2 | D2 | D3 | D3 | D4 | D4 | D5 | D5 | D6 | D6 |
|---|---|---|---|---|---|---|---|---|---|---|---|---|
| 16.03.09 | 3 | 2 | 5 | 0 | 3 | 2 | 5 | 0 | 3 | 2 | 3 | 2 |
| 23.03.09 | 2 | 3 | 4 | 1 | 5 | 0 | 4 | 1 | 4 | 1 | 4 | 1 |
| 01.04.09 | 0 | 5 | 4 | 1 | 4 | 1 | 3 | 2 | 5 | 0 | 3 | 2 |
| 15.04.09 | 2 | 3 | 1 | 4 | 2 | 3 | 5 | 0 | 5 | 0 | 3 | 2 |

The registration counts only the basic form of the dessin.

# Day 1 part session 2

## Curriculum                Break of as a Peak via 2 cushions

The object ball must pass the pin area and end in the 8. part of the table following the pin area.
It must stop as a directly useable direct or an across.
The tempo of the queue ball must make it easily useable on a subsequent direct or, in a combination with object ball 2 as peak via 2 or 4 cushions.

All breaks-off's, which does not meet the above criteria's, are to be counted as errors. Even if there is a score in the shot.

After an approved execution of the break off, continue the series with 4 scoring shots more. Then make a new break-off.
Execute 10 break off's.

Register the number of approved break off's + the number of shots in the subsequent series.

| Date | # OK break-off's | # error break-off's | # OK b.o. but too short series |
|---|---|---|---|
| 17.03.09 | 3 | 8 | 6 |
| 23.03.09 | 3 | 7 | 4 |
| 01.04.09 | 5 | 5 | 1 |
| 15.04.09 | 5 | 5 | 1 |

# Day 1 part session 3

## Curriculum          Peak via 4 cushions

It is to be played from diamond 10 – 60 on the long cushion.
The object ball must pass the pin area and end in the 8. part of the table
following the pin area.
Start with queue and object ball in a comfortable distance from the long
cushion.

After a correct, executed shot on all 6 diamonds, you should vary the
distance between the balls and the distance to the cushion (if and when time
allows).

Register the number of approved attempts per. diamond.
Execute 5 attempts per. diamond

D = Diamond, 1=10, 2=20 etc.

| Date.. | D1 | D1 | D2 | D2 | D3 | D3 | D4 | D4 | D5 | D5 | D6 | D6 |
|---------|----|----|----|----|----|----|----|----|----|----|----|----|
| 17.03.09 | 2 | 3 | 3 | 2 | 2 | 3 | 5 | 0 | 2 | 3 | 3 | 2 |
| 23.03.09 | 4 | 1 | 3 | 2 | 2 | 3 | 4 | 1 | 5 | 0 | 4 | 1 |
| 01.04.09 | 4 | 1 | 3 | 2 | 1 | 4 | 3 | 2 | 5 | 0 | 2 | 3 |
| 15.04.09 | 2 | 3 | 2 | 3 | 2 | 3 | 5 | 0 | 3 | 2 | 4 | 1 |

The registration counts only the basic form of the dessin.

# Day 1 part session 4

## Curriculum          Breaks from ideal position

All 3 balls are placed close to the pin area in a most favourable starting position of your own choice

It must be easy to play a direct on the first object ball leading to a direct on the second object ball in the next shot.

Second object ball is then played by a *prick-shot* (a very small shot) to a new direct or a favourable position two shots further away.

The aim is to make as large a break as possible with full ball and tempo control.

**Execute max. 5 breaks.**

Register the number of breaks and the total point score for each break.

| Date... | # of breaks | # points | Average |
|---------|-------------|----------|---------|
| 17.03.09 | 5 | 150 | 30,00 |
| 23.03.09 | 5 | 172 | 34,40 |
| 01.04.09 | 5 | 140 | 28,00 |
| 15.04.09 | 5 | 150 | 30,00 |

Thus continues the Game Plan for day 2 and 3.
With different curriculums, but following the systematic to the point.
Because it works. It adds and increases competences.
You have seen a shortened extract. But I've not juggled with the results in order to convince you with elaborated facts.

## Some final remarks on the Game Plans.

Once you have acquired the necessary knowledge of a trade, it is not a tedious work to make an educational Game Plan.

Neither needs you to be a highly skilled expert regarding true competences for that trade, in order to do coaching, teaching or to be an instructor.

A very good example of the latter you can see in the world of ballet. Here the instructor is very often an used-to-be excellent dancer of high competence. But believe me, he (or she) has all of the skills, knowledge and competences needed to perform a High Quality ballet instruction and choreographic work.

The key issue is knowledge.

I hope (as a matter of fact, I know) that I have given you knowledge about the Knowledge Society through this book.

Have I caused hunger within you, for participating in creating and forming the Knowledge Society in your country as well as the rest of the world, I have done my job well.

We have only sane reasons, even healthy reasons, to want the Knowledge Society. But we have no reasons at all, not to want it and not to have it.

We can only start the necessary tasks too late.

Your truly

Kjeld Reby Løren

# The Concept of Danish 5 Pin Billiard.

The DK5PB is the most popular billiard game in Denmark. It is the billiard game played by most organized players at all. A variety of the game – Shoemaker (Skomager) is played by thousands of people every day mostly at bars and pubs. But it is also played in many other different places. The most significant difference between the two games is, that Shoemaker is a one shot game with any number of participants.

The DK5PB is played on a table with the same size and much like the table used for all the different kind of carambole disciplines. But like the pool and snooker tables it has 6 pockets. The pockets in the pool and snooker tables are designed to bee "catching". This is not the case for the DK5PB billiard tables.

The best known similar, internationally played game is the International 5 Pin also known as Casino. This is also a game with 5 small pins. Like the Danish Shoemaker it is also a one shot game. But – it has no pockets, and the rules are very different from the DK5PB.

The most obvious difference is though the size of the pins used in DK5PB. They are about 5 times the height of the Casino pins and made of wood. And again of course the 6 pockets

This is the standard DK5PB table. (The 2 strings and the gadget to the right are used in an education session)

You make a score by knocking over the pins and/or make a carambole. Each player uses the same cue ball – the red. The two other balls are normally white. But it could easily be a white and a yellow ball. In case of using two white balls one of them must be marked with a black spot. This is just for assisting the referee in deciding whether a carambole is made..

Each knocked over pin in a shot counts for 2 points. The true carambole counts for 4 points. This gives a maximum of 14 possible points in one shot.

Carambole between the two white balls or pocketing a white ball counts for nothing but is not a fault.

In order to avoiding the game to be a carambole game, the player is only allowed two consecutive, clean caramboles in a row. Then at least one pin must be involved. A clean carambole is counted for as if a cushion was hit.

To make it less boring for the audience, one of the balls must hit a cushion at least every second shot.

A player may (and shall) continue as long as he/she is scoring. In case of a no score or a fault, the next player is in turn. There are no penalties.

The most common faults are pins knocked over by the cue ball or pocketing the cue call.

The game is continued until one of the players has reached the agreed distance (total score). If the game breaking player is the first to reach the distance, the second player is allowed to try to make as high a score as possible from a break off shot. This opens a possibility for a draw.

Most of the games today are played as a one set game. The elite players go for a distance of 800 points.

Now – why isn't this already an international game?

There is one major reason for this: The 6 pockets.

Every 3CC (3 Cushion Carambole) player knows that the pockets are placed on strategically very important places. They exclude the skilled use of many brilliant score and positioning shots.

So – why are they there?

This seems mainly to be a question of history. But there is a far more justifying reason: They are an important challenge in the game. They force the players to take them into account in deciding an actual dessin.

It has been tried in Denmark, to play the DK5PB on normal carambole tables. This was not a success. Some found the game to be too easy. But most players saw and felt that exactly the pockets were one of the inspiring challenges in the game.

As you probably already know, almost all kinds of carambole disciplines have enforced obstructive rules in order to make the games more challenging. The only exception that I can think of is the 3CC.

In order to be able to play the DK5PB on a standard carambole table, I have constructed some artificial pockets. They can be installed and removed in 30 seconds. But more important – they do no harm to the table. Nor do they leave any traces at all. But most important is the fact, that this gives the opportunity to play the DK5PB all over the world by the Danish rules.

But why is that of any important interest?

***Because DK5PB is the second to none best way of learning the fundamentals of any kind of billiard.***

It is true, that the nature of the game is mostly to score by knocking over the pins by the object ball – the second ball. But far more important is the execution of the shot, and thereby positioning both the cue ball and the object ball for a light, floating, continuing game.

Prior to actually executing a shot, the player must evaluate the table for deciding the most suitable dessin. Here is scoring only half part of the goal.

Placing the involved balls at positive positions for the continuation is equally important.

Elements as tempo, draw, follow, English etc. are to be taken into considerations.

Other important factors are, that the effect of the contact between the cue ball and the object ball must be mastered. The same goes for the effect of the contact between the balls and the cushions. And the contact between the object ball and the pins.

You must also know when and how to use the carambole. And in mastering the game you will use free carambole as well as any number of cushions in a carambole. All for the best forwarding play.

DK5PB is containing a multiple number of so called standard dessins or standard balls. These are like tools that you can choose between in solving a situation on the table. Your choice will be to pick the best tool for the actual, presented situation. Sometimes 2 or more tools can be almost equally well suited for a given situation. This gives you the opportunity to play in accordance with your own temperament.

All of the standard balls have a unique name. The name is given by the object balls path to the pin area. There are off course as of today only Danish names for these standard balls. But I have made a list of the most of them and tried to give them English names:

- Direct        OB goes directly into the pin area without touching a cushion first.
- Peak          OB goes through short and long cushion into the pin area.

- Double Peak    OB goes through short, long, short and long cushion into the pin area.
- Across    OB goes through long cushion into the pin area.
- Double across    OB goes through long and long cushion into the pin area.
- Long    OB goes through short cushion into the pin area.
- Double Long    OB goes through short and short cushion into the pin area.
- Quarter    OB goes through long, short and long cushion into the pin area.
- High Peak    OB goes through long and short cushion into the pin area.

There are a few more, but the above listed are the most commonly used in a game.

An objective of the game is to position all 3 balls in the outer or inner pin area. The outer area is a square between the 2 Salvo lines (a centered quadrant square with the size of half the table). The inner area is a quadrant square with the size of 2 by 2 diamonds (an 8-part of the table) around the pins. Doing so makes scoring and control of the balls much easier. The opposite requires undesirable long ball paths.

I am trying to enforce the view of a billiard player as a crafts man. Learning the specific kind of game is like an education for a smith, a carpenter etc. This is for most players a completely new approach. It makes the process of learning a much more serious business. But strangely enough – also easier. How?

The player is presented with a complete job description for a skilled DK5PB player. This is a head line listing of all the elements that must be mastered. Included is both the physical skills but also psychology and mental skills. All of this is put into the total education program. So – upfront – the player sees a clear, visual goal and a path to success.

In the next step - in setting up an education - the job description is broken down into a detail job description. Now we move from headlines towards exact, measureable skill details. These are partly or short term goals. These details can be put into actual learning schemes known as Game Plans.

The total education is made up of many Game Plans. A Game Plan has a relatively short time span.

Game Plans are 3-step modules: Instruction, training and evaluation.

- In step 1 the coach gives all the information about a detail element. This could be for instance the standard Peak ball. Information such as how, when and why to use it is given. The full variants of the element are demonstrated by the coach. The coach makes sure, that all information is both given and understood. The student then starts the training supervised by the coach.

- In step 2 the students do the training mostly by themselves. At all times the coach can be consulted.
  Training consists of clearly defined exercises. There is an accurate setup of the balls. Target definitions for the result of the shots are given. And the result is recorded.
  The recording consists of: Date, exercise, times executed, times successfully.

- In step 3 the coach performs an evaluation. All the students' recordings for the Game Plan is examined. The coach then decides whether all exercises are learned and mastered sufficiently successful. The next Game Plan is then set up. This will consist of exercises from the former Game Plan that need further training plus new education and exercises.

In this way runs the total education mixed with elements of psychology and mental education. Relaxed sessions of informal conversation between the coach and the students are placed at appropriate intervals. The coach needs to assure, that the students at all times are comfortable and are confident in what they are doing. That they feel safe and in good hands.

At certain intervals the coach set up gathering evaluations. This is done to assure, that knowledge gained earlier are not lost or forgotten.

At the end of all education the final examination is performed. It falls in 2 categories: The soft values and the technical values.

- The soft values is a number of question and answer issues. The examiner asks questions about the students feeling of his/her own attitudes towards and abilities in a number of issues. The answers are the student's best guesses. The student cannot fail on the soft part.

- The technical values looks very much like one large Game Plan. It covers most of the materials learned throughout the education. Each little exercise is given max. 3 attempts. At the end the whole examination is evaluated. If at least 80 % of the exercises are done successfully the student has passed. He or she can now call themselves a fully educated DK5PB player. The graduation is confirmed by a signed certificate.

Most likely the final examination has shown some gaps of knowledge or skills. This gives the coach and the player the opportunity to set up a Game Plan for closing these gaps. Whether the student will use this Game Plan or not is up to him or her. But it is an extra service from the coach.

The above education is scheduled for a student with no preceding knowledge.

Kjeld Reby Løren
Syrenvej 10 A
Ellinge Lyng
DK4560 Vig
Denmark

| | |
|---|---|
| Telephone | +45 40 89 67 99 |
| Email | akloeren@privat.dk |
| WEB | kjeldloeren.mono.net (a totally Danish site) |

**Two pages for your own notes:**